ADVENTURES
AFTER 50

To Amy

" Go For It "

Judy & Don

ADVENTURES AFTER 50

✦

Doing More Than You Ever Thought You Could

Don and Judy Mac Isaac

iUniverse, Inc.
New York Lincoln Shanghai

ADVENTURES AFTER 50
Doing More Than You Ever Thought You Could

iUniverse books may be ordered through booksellers or by contacting:

iUniverse
2021 Pine Lake Road, Suite 100
Lincoln, NE 68512
www.iuniverse.com
1-800-Authors (1-800-288-4677)

ISBN-13: 978-0-595-41015-6 (pbk)
ISBN-13: 978-0-595-85368-7 (ebk)
ISBN-10: 0-595-41015-4 (pbk)
ISBN-10: 0-595-85368-4 (ebk)

Printed in the United States of America

Contents

ACKNOWLEDGMENTS

Writing this book was an adventure in its own right, and it was clear early on that we needed intelligent and timely feedback. To that end, I asked a few writer friends whose judgment I respect to read some of the chapters. Pete Hillyer, Chuck Francis, Cliff Jenks, Richard Atcheson, David Noland, and Bob Gilbert were quick to respond with thoughtful and helpful comments. For that, I thank them.

Thanks also to Dave Thomas, computer consultant, who kept our computer up and running when we needed help—which was often. And lastly, to our children, Cathy, Mike, and Cameron: You were our first adventure. Thanks for your patience.

THE LIST

√ 1   Parachute from an airplane

√ 2   Raft the Colorado River rapids

√ 3   Get SCUBA certification

√ 4   Attend the Olympic Games

√ 5   Start a business

√ 6   Go on an African safari

√ 7   Climb Mount Kilimanjaro

√ 8   Write and be published

√ 9   Fly in a hot air balloon

√ 10 Speak in public

√ 11 Parasail

   12 Hang glide

√ 13 Fly a glider

√ 14 Learn to rock climb

   15 Climb the Matterhorn

   16 Learn to play piano

√ 17 Raft the Bío Bío River (Chilé)

   18 Go down the Amazon River

   19 Climb Mount Aconcagua (Andes)

√ 20 Learn CPR

√ 21 Trek in Nepal and see Mount Everest

√ 22 Learn to "jitterbug"

   23 Play the harmonica

√ 24 Go dog sledding

√ 25 Fly in an open cockpit biplane

   26 Learn to cartoon

√ 27 Explore Antarctica

√ 28 Go kayaking

   29 See Australia

   30 Learn to juggle

   31 Climb Mount Fuji (at eighty)

√ Completed

PROLOGUE

Have you ever thought of doing something exciting in your life? Or at least something different, like climbing a tall mountain, running white-water rapids in a rubber raft, or even parachuting from an airplane? There are things many of us dream about but seldom do.

Reaching my fiftieth year, I realized that something was missing. Here I was thundering toward old age and had never fulfilled any of the side-tracked dreams of my youth. Down deep, I knew that if I didn't get started soon, I never would. So I listed thirty-one goals I had always wanted to reach and showed the list to my wife, Judy. She was skeptical of some of the goals, but she liked the overall idea and agreed to join me on many of the trips.

It's important to note that Judy and I are not wealthy. We knew that we would have to prepare for this new lifestyle by saving for it. Our three kids were in college at the time, but that financial burden would be lifted in about three years when they graduated.

We both joined a health club and began taking hikes in the mountains near our home. Soon we were using weekends, holidays, and vacation time to increase our fitness. Within six months, we could see some progress.

In the years to follow, we reached twenty-one of the original thirty-one goals and traveled to places that we could not have imagined earlier. To Judy's surprise (and delight), she accomplished many of the goals and, in this book, talks about them from her point of view.

We knew at the outset that some goals would be too expensive, too dangerous, or too time-consuming. But we didn't know which ones. And that was OK. We'd find out soon enough what could or couldn't be done. What was important at that moment was to *start*.

Start the journey.

PARACHUTING

I was fifty-one. A year had passed since I made my list of goals, and I had dawdled. At least I had begun talking to people about parachuting from an airplane. Progress of a sort, I rationalized. Then I talked to a colleague of mine who had parachuted. "Parachuting's no big deal. All you have to do is fall out of the airplane. Just do it!" he said dismissively.

Signing up for parachuting was not difficult, but truth be known, I was afraid of wimping out. What if I got up there and couldn't jump? Just froze?

I checked into scheduling it and to my surprise, discovered that I could jump on the same day I trained. "Hey!" I thought, "Maybe my friend was right. It might not be as hard as I thought." And I would use only one vacation day from work. Warming to the idea, I thought, "What better way to start the list than to go for a difficult goal?"

I decided to parachute.

The drop zone was at the Lakewood Parachute Center (which is no longer in operation) in Lakewood, New Jersey. It was about two hours south of New York City, close to the New Jersey shore. The center had a good reputation for safety, an important consideration for a would-be parachutist.

As the big day approached, I was surprisingly calm. But then, that very week, I read a newspaper article about a student being killed on his first jump in upstate New York. He had panicked, grabbed the edge of his chute, and held it like a security blanket all the way down.

"Whoa!" I thought. I was concerned, but I was also aware that, of the estimated two million Americans who scuba dive every year, there are approximately one hundred deaths, according to SCUBA Diving Safely. In 2003 there were 622 bicycling fatalities resulting from traffic crashes, according to the Bicycling Information Center. The dropzone.com skydiving database reported sixty nine skydiving fatalities in 2004 and fifty nine fatalities in 2005.

Class began at 10:00 AM with an hour-long lecture. There were seven of us in the class. The others, decades younger than me, ranged in age from their early twenties to late thirties. Christine, the only woman in the group, was short, blond, and perky. She seemed very focused—the kind of person who, when she made up her mind to do something, did it. She was with a guy named Charlie—a friend or husband—who appeared to be the least athletic person in the group. He was short and overweight, with a receding hairline. Charlie talked non-stop. He was either trying to impress Christine or dispel his own fears about the jump. *"Whistling by the graveyard,"* I thought.

Lee, our instructor, was tall, trim, and dark-haired. He was a little cocky, and his pleasant demeanor changed curt when someone who didn't answer his questions. He had all the makings of a Marine drill sergeant, I thought.

We learned how to exit the aircraft, arching our backs so that our descent would be belly-down or face-to-earth, as it was called. We were told that, with our arms and legs arched behind us, our bellies would literally force our bodies into a horizontal position, facing the ground.

We also learned how to operate the chute after it opened, and what to do if it didn't. Lee told us if our parachutes didn't open, we were to get rid of the main chute. To do that, we were to unsnap two-hinged metal plates near each shoulder on the harness, revealing two thick, wire rings. Our thumbs went into the rings and pulled hard, cutting the main chute loose. Then, just as quickly, we were to place our left hands over the reserve chute and, with our right hands, pull the ripcord handle to expose the chute. If we weren't fast enough, the reserve chute would not open automatically, and we would have to pull the chute out of its pack *manually.* We would have to raise the chute over our right shoulders, and throw it out in the direction of our spin. The chute would deploy into a life-saving canopy. And if that didn't work, we were told to pull the chute back, and throw it again. Indeed, keep throwing it, we were told, until it opened. (*Or I was planted in New Jersey sod,* I thought.) The procedure sounded logical, but I had trouble envisioning such a cool-headed performance while falling at one hundred miles an hour.

During a break, I talked to a young guy named Spencer, who appeared nervous and stuttered a bit.

"I bet a guy fifty dollars I could do this," he said. "He was bustin' my chops about being afraid, and I got sick of it." He paused a moment. "There were people around when I bet him, so now I gotta do it."

After the break we went to the jumping pits, where, for an hour and a half, we jumped onto sandy ground from a four-foot-high wooden platform. The landing shock from a jump out of an airplane, we were told, was about equal to leaping off a small flat-bed truck traveling five miles an hour. Not bad, I thought.

We learned how to fall, with our knees bent and feet together, and how to roll on our side to absorb the impact.

"You can break a leg," Lee said, "if your feet aren't together." To simulate landings, we jumped from a smaller platform, trying front, back, and side positions to learn different approaches depending on the wind. When a chute opened, one's forward speed, we were told, should be about eight miles per hour. But, if there were a ten-mile-an-hour wind, the forward speed at landing would be eighteen miles per hour. Much too fast. So procedure called for turning the chute into the wind so the forward speed would off-set the wind speed, resulting in an ideal landing speed of about two miles per hour.

Our jump plane was a small blue and white Cessna 180. I had hoped for the larger DC-3 that I understood the center owned. That would have enabled a more dramatic exit, I thought (like yelling *Geronimo* or something), but, alas, the DC-3 was being repaired. Oh, well.

Lee explained how three students, the pilot, and himself would wedge into the plane; how we would exit; and in what order we would jump. He instructed us to move slowly to keep our reserve chute handle from catching on something and opening automatically.

Then it was back to the jumping pits to practice our exits and what he called "the all-important arch," a procedure to insure that our chutes cleared the plane. We used another platform that simulated the Cessna's stair and wing strut. Lee showed us how to push off with our feet, which are stronger than our hands (which I had trouble doing). He had each of us count aloud "arch one thousand, arch two thousand" on up to five thousand. "By that time," he said, "the chute should be deployed by the static line.

"If it doesn't open, consider it a malfunction," Lee barked, "and immediately pull the ripcord on the reserve chute! You hear? Immediately!"

One at a time, we practiced our exits in the jump pit.

"Arch one thousand," I shouted.

"I can't hear you!" yelled Lee.

"Two thousand, three thousand!" I yelled louder.

"Four thousand, five thousand …"

"It's a good chute!" shouted Lee. "Whatta ya do?"

"Reach for the toggle handles and pull for the target!" I yelled back.

"You're at the perimeter of the target, and the wind is going to blow you over it! Whatta ya do?"

"Pull the toggle all the way down and turn my chute into the wind!"

And so it went, with Lee shouting imaginary situations at each of us to check our responses until they were reflexive. After three hours of reacting to all the things that could go wrong, I began to wonder if anything would go right.

Class was over. We were issued helmets, jump-suits, and two parachutes, main and reserve. Lee and another instructor strapped us into the parachutes and attached a radio receiver to our reserve chute for ground-to-air communication. The main chute was nylon with a standard round canopy of twenty-eight feet. It weighed ten pounds. Both were strapped so tightly around me I could barely walk. *A sumo wrestler with parachute*—came to mind. And, while I might get my feet together for a landing, I thought, there was no way my knees would ever meet.

I was to be in the first of two plane-loads of students and would jump second after Spencer. Irving, also on his first jump, would go third. As we lumbered toward the plane, reality set in. *My God, this is it,* I thought. *In less than fifteen minutes, I'm going to jump out of this dinky little plane from twenty-five-hundred feet.* At that moment, it seemed like the dumbest thing I had ever done.

Irving, who wasn't saying much, fit sideways into the tail section of the plane. He would jump last (lucky dog). I wedged in behind the pilot. Spencer was next to the door. Lee, now on his knees between Spencer and Irving, would direct our exits. As soon as Lee shut the door, the pilot started the engine, and the plane went from the shortest taxi-run in aviation history to a roaring take-off. We were airborne.

No one talked except Lee, who was giving directions to the pilot. Each of us had our own thoughts. With some apprehension, I looked out the window and saw the target below—a giant chalk circle, eight hundred feet in diameter.

After a few minutes, the pilot dryly announced on the intercom that we were now at jump altitude. Lee opened the door and, instantly, a blast of seventy-mile-an-hour air rushed into the cabin. Until then, it had seemed like we were cruising along at about forty miles per hour. But with the door open, the loud engine, and the rushing wind, we all knew that the moment had arrived. Lee, who was now ordering Spencer into position. He was all business.

As I watched Spencer slowly edge his legs outside the door, I asked myself, *What the hell am I doing here?* I felt like an actor from an old World War II movie. Only this was different: I wasn't *looking* at a movie. I *was* the movie.

"Ready!" Lee yelled at Spencer. At this point, part of me didn't want to watch. But another part—the morbid, curious part, did. Spencer's feet were now wedged on the wooden step just below the open door, his hands locked on the wing strut. Looking at Lee, his eyes seemed much larger than I remembered in class.

Before I could ponder the thought, Lee yelled to the pilot to slow air speed; then he slapped Spencer's leg and yelled again.

"Go!"

Spencer was gone.

With hardly a pause, Lee turned around and looked at me (almost malevolently, I thought).

"Mac Isaac, into position!" he ordered. I almost wanted to ask, *"Isn't it a bit windy for jumping today?"* But I didn't have that kind of courage.

Sliding reluctantly toward the open door was like an out-of-body experience. It seemed that I hadn't really moved at all. I thought of myself as still cowering behind the pilot's seat, watching this gray-haired guy (me) sliding his butt toward the open door.

The plane re-circled the target. I was now sitting on the edge of the open door, all but frozen with fear. I felt the full force of the air speed. My legs were blowing like wind socks toward the tail of the plane. As instructed by Lee, I slowly reached for the wing strut with my left hand. It had been so easy on the ground; now it was a test of strength, as if the wind dared me to reach the strut. The wind was so strong that I had trouble planting my feet on the small wooden stair. In the air, it looked about the size of a Hershey bar. Finally, I got both feet on the stair. With my right hand, I reached through the gale and grabbed the upper part of the strut and slowly pulled myself up and out.

I was now completely outside the aircraft, standing on this dumb little stair, leaning into an incredible wind. I was sure that, within seconds, I'd blow away. Now I understood Lee's earlier comment: "Holding on to the wing strut is easy. It's letting go that's hard."

"Ready?" Lee barked at me. *My God, he's really going to do it,* I thought. Another image flashed through my mind: *This must have been what it was like to be a wing walker in the old barnstorming days of aviation.*

The next few seconds were a blur. I didn't hear Lee shout, "Go!", but he slapped my leg to convey the same order. I let go. I don't recall yelling anything heroic like "arch one thousand, arch two thousand." It was more like "*Aaaaaarrrggghh!*"

What I do recall, however, was dropping down and away from the aircraft at a frightfully dizzying speed. I saw the plane's tail as it flew away from my exit point in the sky. Then, finally, that glorious feeling of the chute opening, with its a welcome jerk on my shoulders. Only then did my brain kick in. I looked up at the chute. My beautiful chute. *I love it! I love it! No malfunction. Thank you, God!* The worst was over. *I'm not going to die*, I thought. Even though I had another two thousand feet to descend, my fear was gone.

I reached for the toggle handles that would steer my chute to the target. I pulled the right handle, and the chute turned right. *Hey, this really works*, I thought. Looking down through my feet. I saw what appeared to be people near a small truck. Mere specks on the ground.

I now moved the right toggle so that I'd be heading for the center of the target. *Wouldn't it be great*, I thought, *if I could land dead center?* Confidence soaring, I luxuriated in the view. Spectacular. Beyond the Garden State Parkway, I could see some little border towns along the New Jersey shore and the Atlantic Ocean. *Aerial postcards*, I thought. *What a high!*

I was also aware of the stillness and my own breathing as I floated to earth. Even though the descent would last only about three minutes, the feeling was euphoric, something I had never experienced before.

Suddenly, my thoughts were interrupted by a sharp voice on my radio.

"Don, you're looking good. Pull the left toggle." I did and, sure enough, the chute headed into a mild wind to edge me closer to the target. The figures on the ground were now getting larger, and I knew I should be thinking about landing. Indeed, the ground was coming at me faster than I had expected. I remembered Lee saying, *Don't look down, look at the horizon! You can't judge your rate of descent.*

I could see Spencer on the ground with the instructor who was talking to me on the radio. They were coming at me fast. *Better get ready*, I thought. I looked at the horizon, put my feet together, bent my knees and waited.

BLAM!

The landing wasn't too hard, but it certainly wasn't soft. I had the distinct impression that the ground was unwilling to concede anything. As instructed in class, I rolled gracelessly on my side and scrambled up on my feet to grab my canopy—now billowing in the wind in its effort to escape again (and drag me with it). Finally, the chute collapsed into submission. It was over.

I had made my first parachute jump!

Adrenaline flowed. I was pumped. I congratulated Spencer on his jump and for winning his bet. I excitedly asked inane questions of the instructor who completely ignored me because he was busy talking Irving down. I thought Irving hit hard, but Spencer disagreed. "No different than yours," he said. *So much for landing superiority*, I thought.

With the exception of Charley, who landed somewhere in the woods, but safely, the rest of the class successfully completed their jumps on, or close to, target. Soon we were all trudging back to the administration building to exchange our jumpsuits for civilian gear.

On the long drive home, I lowered my car window and yelled at the wind, just as loudly as I could. Seemed like the right thing to do.

RUNNING the COLORADO RIVER

When our kids were young, Judy and I took them on a trip across the United States so they could see what their country looked like. We covered over seventy five hundred miles in twenty two states in a car pulling a trailer. Cathy was fourteen; Michael, twelve; and Cameron, eight. It was a great trip, and the highlight for all of us, we later agreed, was the Grand Canyon, one of the Seven Natural Wonders of the World. Our first reaction on seeing it from the rim was stunned silence, bordering on reverence. As I stared, something caught my eye. It was a *raft.* On the Colorado

River. I watched it for a while, riveted. All I could think of was how great it must be to see the canyon from that perspective. At that moment, I vowed that one day we would go down the Colorado River in a raft.

Ten years later, Judy and I returned to the canyon. This time we were at the village on the south rim. We packed our duffel bags and prepared for our descent to the canyon floor the next morning. We had signed up for an eight-day trip that would cover 139 of the 226 miles of the river that winds its way through Arizona. Our journey would start at Phantom Ranch and end at Diamond Creek, not far from where the river empties into Lake Mead in Nevada. We had to make reservations ten months in advance because the National Park Service limits the number of people in the canyon at any one time. Moreover, anything brought into the canyon (including waste) has to be taken out to protect the canyon's delicate ecosystem.

To get there, we flew from New York to Las Vegas and, the following day, took a commuter flight directly over the canyon. The view was stunning. The Grand Canyon is a mile deep in many places, 277 miles in length, and anywhere from less than a mile to eighteen miles across. The river's flow, which began to form the canyon six million years ago, etches through the rock with sand and lime, hollowing out some eighty thousand tons of soil every twenty-four hours. That soil then flows down the river. It's considered the best example of water erosion in the world today. (Source: *New York Times*)

From our small plane, we could see the river snaking its way around the canyon floor. We also saw the only Indian reservation in the canyon. The Havasupai tribe consists of some two hundred people who grow their own food—primarily grain, fruit, and vegetables. When necessary, they can reach the nearest town by horseback for medicine and other essentials.

After packing our duffel bags, we brought them to the mule station near our hotel, where mules would carry them down the winding, ten-mile Bright Angel Trail the following morning. We could have arranged to go down on mule-back ourselves, but chose to hike down and pick up our bags at Phantom Ranch, where we would meet our guides. Knowing that our hike would take five hours, we got to bed early. We had been warned to leave before dawn, since temperatures on the canyon floor can easily reach over one hundred degrees Fahrenheit by noon.

The descent was tough. After four hours under a broiling sun, our muscles ached and our feet hurt. By the time we arrived at Phantom Ranch an hour later, our legs were numb, and we felt incapable of taking another step. *Hardly heroic figures*, I thought, as I began wondering if this trip was such a great idea.

The scene greeting us at the Phantom Ranch was one of confusion and noise. At first, we couldn't tell the guides from the passengers. Gear was being unloaded for people who were leaving their rafts after a six-day trip, while fresh supplies were being loaded for those of us who were starting an eight-day trip, and who were ready to climb aboard. There were six eighteen-foot rubber rafts in our flotilla. Four of them would carry people (three or four passengers and a guide per raft). Two rafts were designated to carry provisions for the trip. After everything was finally stowed in the rafts, we put on our life jackets and pushed off. We were on the river.

To avoid capsizing, a raft needs to be balanced, and to achieve this, the guide usually sits in the middle of the raft to row, perched on metal boxes of gear. The boxes and the metal, waterproof "ammo" cans that hold cameras, film, and other valuables provide weight that help with balance. Passengers (usually three) will sit on the bench directly in front of the guide. A fourth seat in the stern can be used when running the more moderate rapids. The black bags containing all our gear, are stowed directly behind the guide.

Judy: Those ubiquitous black bags were intimidating at first. Made from a rubberized, waterproof fabric, they were slightly larger than a king-sized pillowcase. Each person got one. In the bag, you kept all your clothing and needs for the trip. We did have small "ammo" cans—rectangular boxes which could be strapped to the raft to carry items you'd need during the day in the raft, such as sunglasses, suntan lotion, and cameras. I never gave a thought to how everything would be carried through those tumultuous rapids and stay dry. I just knew a suitcase would never do.

We eventually became quite adept at rolling clothes compactly and "getting everything battened down." One of the guides taught us to sit on the bags as they were being packed to squeeze all the air out. Don and I learned to work as a team: I folded, Don stuffed, and I sat. It was amazing what they carried in our little flotilla. Naturally there was a bag of medical emergency equipment plus all of our tents, tarps for the kitchen in case it rained, all of the fresh and frozen food to feed this hungry gang for eight days. And we ate well. Besides dinners and hearty breakfasts, the guides would surprise us with a fresh fruit salad in a watermelon shell for lunch. They made ice cream one hot day. They brought along dishes, silverware, cooking pans, and a table to serve it on. Of course there was a well stocked emergency kit.

The guides told us to *always* hold on to the safety-line that encircles the raft while on the river. If we didn't, they said, we could fall out of the raft into the rapids. The message was not lost on any of us.

There were twenty-two of us in our group: Sixteen passengers and six guides. Most of our fellow adventurers were from California, including a couple of youthful surfers; a young medical doctor and his wife; an environmental director a recent divorcé; and four engineers, three of whom worked at TRW, and the fourth, McDonnell Aircraft. Also among our raft-mates were two professional skiers, an attorney from Colorado, and a supermarket owner from Bremen, Germany, who was realizing his dream of a lifetime. Judy and I were the only delegates from the East. Our lead guide, Greg, told us that we'd usually be on the river for five or six hours a day and would sleep in our sleeping bags along the river edge at night.

In the raft with Judy and me were Herb, an environmental director from California, and Barbara, who was "looking for a little excitement" after a recent divorce. She didn't have to wait long. Greg alerted us that we were approaching Horn Creek, our first rapid.

"This is an 'eight,' so get ready for some action," he said quietly.

The Colorado River classifies their rapids on a one to ten scale, with ten being the most difficult.

About then, we began to hear a roar like a freight train. Looking up we saw the cause: angry, churning, brown rapids that appeared to be clambering for the sky.

"Grip the safety line," Greg told us. "And lean forward so our bow doesn't tip."

Despite the warnings, Judy and I were not ready for that first whack of cold water. It hit us with surprising force and came from all directions. We were instantly soaked by some of the coldest water I had ever experienced. The raft was riding up, over, and through five-and six-foot high waves for what seemed like minutes, but was only seconds. Then, suddenly, our bow stood at a dangerously sharp angle. *My God, it's going to capsize,* I thought.

"Bail!" Greg yelled, "Bail!"

The raft was filling with water, making it hard for him to row. The rest of us were trying to bail with buckets, but we were slipping on the wet raft bottom. (Most rafts today are self-bailing.) With powerful strokes, Greg rowed for the "tongue," a small confluence of stable water between rapids. Eventually we got the hang of it and bailed for all we were worth. And so we were christened, exhilarated, and very wet. The last condition would soon be corrected by a hot canyon sun.

After a series of less difficult rapids and a few miles of floating, it was time to make our first camp along a sandy shore. It was then that we got better acquainted with Greg, our trip leader, and the other guides.

Greg, was a big man—well over six feet and muscular. His black beard and quick smile dominated a constantly animated face. He liked jokes and puzzles, as some of us would soon find out. Greg was a good leader, fully aware of his responsibilities and the trip's demanding schedule. Even more important, he knew when to laugh and relax.

The other guides were Jeff, Chris, Ann, Butch, and Scott. Jeff was a fun-loving, muscular, red-bearded veteran of white-water rapids around the world. Chris was a bright young man, also bearded, who, when not rafting, taught music in San Francisco. His rich, baritone voice would awaken us at 5:30 AM to start our day. Ann, our only female guide, was a little over five feet, attractive, with short, blond hair.

Butch and Scott were apprentice guides, responsible for the two rafts with our provisions. Butch was tall and lanky; Scott, shorter. Neither carried an ounce of fat on them. Both had beards. Apprentice guides cannot take people rafting on the Colorado until they have successfully navigated the river three times without people. This would be the third time for each of them.

Judy: I enjoyed meeting Ann. Having a female guide as part of the team was a plus. Why is it easier sometimes to relate to women than men? Ann was feminine, but she held her own with her male counterparts whenever hard work was required. After a strenuous day in the raft, she'd often change into a skirt and blouse as she worked with the other guides preparing food for the evening meal. She also made a mean guacamole dip (her mother's recipe, she said.)

The guides alternated responsibilities, so no one ever had tasks they disliked for a long stretch, and someone always had an evening off. They worked well as a team. I was surprised at the number of women traveling—some spouses, some singles, some in groups, and all out to have a good time. This was the first of the adventure trips Don and I took, so I didn't know what to expect. But we were to find women—whether girls fresh out of college or groups of women out for adventure—traveling in large numbers on just about all of our trips., from two girls fresh out of college who wanted to see a bit of the world, before settling down, to single women not content to stay home and let the world pass them by, to groups of women just out to have an adventure. One good-natured lady on our trip to Nepal confessed to being in her eighties. She never turned down an optional side trip, even when that meant climbing through rough terrain. And she was always there at cocktail time with many interesting stories to tell of her life.

One major plus when traveling in these tour groups—from a woman's point of view—is that we always felt safe, as long as we listened to our guides' instructions and stayed with the group.

On our first night, each of us was issued something called a "tube tent." It was essentially a piece of plastic, about eight feet long and four feet wide. The idea was for each of us to shape this piece of plastic into a miniature tent (tube) that could be strung by a rope and tied at either end to tree branches or large rocks. However, there weren't enough trees or rocks to go around, so we had to improvise. But that was OK. We made do.

Our first night in camp proved to be a model for what would follow: Guides cooked the meals on portable gas stoves, and they were good cooks. There was an informal cocktail hour with guides supplying hors d'oeuvres, beer, and soft drinks, plus whatever "spirits" people had brought along with them. It was a chance to relax and talk to our new companions. Dinner that night included steak, garlic bread, salad, and dessert. Breakfasts might include ham and eggs, English muffins, blueberry pancakes, fruit, juice, coffee, tea, and hot chocolate. We ate a lot.

On our second day, Judy and I shared a raft with Rob and Cindy, the young surfers from California. They were an attractive couple, probably in their late twenties. Cindy was Asian American and a trifle shy. Rob was quite a bit taller, and his chiseled torso suggested that he worked out regularly. Both were trim and athletic. They traveled the world looking for excitement. Their mantra: adventure now, family later.

Setting up camp

The next day, we were on the river by eight o'clock and, within forty minutes, reached our first maelstrom of the day, Granite Rapid. As would be the pattern for all major rapids, we secured rafts upstream. The guides checked out the conditions we'd be facing that day by climbing rock above the rapid and visually assessing the conditions. No matter how many times a guide has run a particular rapid, he makes no assumptions. Water levels can change overnight, for a variety of reasons. Release of water from Glen Canyon Dam, varies depending on demands for electricity. The release amount determines the quantity and depth of the water flow throughout the canyon, which affects how turbulent the rapids are. Rainfall is another major factor.

Our next two rapids, Granite (seven) and Hermit (eight), gave us wild, soaking rides followed by periods of tranquility. While floating downstream, we would often lay back and admire the beauty of the canyon, with its infinite palette of color and rock formations.

We were told that Crystal Rapid, our third of the day, was formed one night in 1966 when a flash flood tumbled boulders from Crystal Creek into the river, creating a narrow gorge. With a nine rating, the rapid is considered by many guides to be one of the river's most treacherous. We thought, having survived our earlier encounters, that we were ready for Crystal. Wrong!

Within seconds of our entrance into the rapid, walls of water crashed into our raft, tossing it like a cork. Again, I was sure we were going to capsize.

"Bail! Bail!" shouted Chris, our guide for the day. As we had learned earlier, it's hard to bail and still keep one's balance, but self-preservation prevailed. It was bail or sink. We bailed.

We passed through the turbulence were once again in calm water. Chris would tell us later that he worries more about Crystal than any other rapid.

"What do you do if we capsize?" someone asked early in the trip. Greg's immediate answer was, "If possible, stay with the raft and, if you can, hold on to the safety line that runs around it. Your life jacket will keep you buoyant until you're swept into calmer waters. The biggest concern is rocks, so keep your feet pointed downriver so you can see what's coming. Then use your feet to push away from the rocks."

Greg said that people had drowned in the canyon, but there had not been deaths recently, due in large measure to the improved quality of the rafts.

"However," Greg said with a wry smile, "there are only two kinds of boatmen: those who have flipped, and those who are going to."

We stopped for lunch at Shinumo Falls, a beautiful but powerful waterfall some forty feet high. We could see a cave at its base, directly behind the sheeting water, so Pat—a young attorney from Colorado—and I had an idea. We thought if we could reach the cave by diving deep enough under the falls to avoid being stunned, we could surface inside the cave. Sounded reasonable, we thought at the time.

Holding our breath, we dove down about twelve feet and immediately began swimming to the surface. As we came up into the mouth of the cave, we were hammered by the waterfall. It was scary. Since we had only one option, we swam as hard as we could, finally surfacing inside the cave. It was a strange sight looking through the waterfall at the outside world. But we were chilled to the bone and breathing heavily. We decided not to dawdle and dove back into the water, eventually resurfacing at our original starting point. It was fun, but once was enough.

That evening we had Chinese food for dinner, an unexpected treat. Indeed, everything seemed to be going well. Almost too well. Then I noticed the guides erecting a large tarpaulin.

"Might have a little rain tonight," Greg said laconically.

He was right. That night we had a downpour.

Judy and I dug a moat and built dikes around the two small tube-tents that we'd been issued. The idea was to divert rainwater away from the tents. But as the rain became heavier, our childlike dikes began to leak, then crumble. We added more dirt, but, by then, the walls were falling. When the rain found its way under our ground cloth, we knew that the battle was over.

Groans and gripes from adjoining tents confirmed that we weren't alone. Flash floods are always a concern on the canyon floor. Heavy rains such as we were experiencing could raise the river several feet in less than an hour, so campsites are always on high ground.

Rainwater was now coming into our tent virtually unchecked, so we had to run for it. Judy and I grabbed blankets, clothing, and flashlights and headed for the tarpaulin. Tripping over rocks and bushes, we reached the shelter of the tarpaulin to discover that we were not alone. Other campers and guides were already there, also soaked and feeling as wretched as we did. As the rain continued, more campers came staggering in from the dark until all but the very few who had their own tents, were under the tarp with us.

The next morning, people slowly awoke to discover that they were sleeping next to people they hardly knew, huddled together like a litter of wet pups. After a hot breakfast, we dried our clothes on sun-heated rocks, and our miseries were gradually forgotten. We were ready to get back on the river.

Again, we were with Barbara and Herb. Our guide was Ann, who wore a jaunty pith helmet for protection against the sun. We hit whitewater immediately, and she handled it ably. Between rapids, we got to know her. Ann told us she loved what she was doing. She ran rivers six months a year and worked as a lab technician the other six. She knew that she was a pioneer for her gender in the sport, and like many of the guides, had no immediate interest in settling down. She was also aware of the problems and dangers. Once, she told us, while traveling in India on her way to a job, she found herself the only woman on a large ferry boat with over four hundred male passengers, all of whom stared at her. The staring didn't bother her as much as discovering that there were no lavatory facilities on board for women.

"Now *that* was a problem!" Ann said.

Later in the day, we saw bighorn sheep leaping from rock to rock in graceful, sure-footed moves. Other wildlife in the canyon include about three hundred species of birds along with beavers, elk, lizards, mountain lions, mule deer, pronghorns, and many snakes. We were advised to check our sneakers every morning in case a scorpion had decided to curl up and spend the night there. Scorpions love damp sneakers.

The next day was Sunday, and while we couldn't attend church as we usually would, we felt we didn't have to. We were already in an outdoor cathedral. The river was calm, and we were floating silently past majestic rock formations. In sharp contrast to the tumult of the previous day, a sense of peace prevailed. No man-made church could have equaled the tranquility of our surroundings.

After several moderate rapids, we tied up at Deer Creek Falls, where we could wash some clothes in the frigid water. We also had a chance for a quick sponge down with a special soap that didn't contaminate the river.

At camps and stops along the way, guides would set up Port-a-Potties, women's upstream and men's downstream. It was a simple system, and it worked.

That night, Judy and I decided to sleep out in the open on a rock ledge under the stars, listening to the nearby waterfalls. Looking at the silhouetted crags and peaks surrounding us, we felt in harmony with the world.

On the morning of our fifth day, Herb, Barbara, Judy, and I (pretty much a foursome now) joined Greg again in his raft. We ran three rapids: Fishtail (four), Kanab (five), and Upset (six). The last got its name in 1923 after Emory Kolb, a geologist, drowned when his dory capsized.

Our group was coming together well enough to allow for a few pranks by the guides. One sting operation involved Homer, one of the engineers from California, was sitting alone in the bow of Christor's raft, gazing hypnotically at the water in front of him.

While he was mesmerized, his three companions quietly crept back into the stern and hid behind a pile of gear. Christor, who was rowing the raft, quietly pulled in his oars and joined the other conspirators in hiding. The only sound was the recurring slap of water against the raft.

When Homer eventually became aware of the silence, he turned around to discover that everyone was gone and he was alone. He panicked, and immediately began shouting loudly, "Help! Help! Everybody fell out of the raft! I'm alone!! Help! Can anybody heeaaarr me?"

When it looked like Homer might go ballistic, his "friends" magically appeared in the stern of the raft, all smiles and laughter. Homer was not amused. He later commented to anyone who would listen, "When we get back to California, I'll get them for this."

The next day, to break routine, we took a seven-mile hike up Havasu Creek to Beaver Falls, one hundred feet above the river. The trail wound through heavy brush and rocky terrain, but our destination made the effort worth it. The Falls were a series of shallow pools at descending levels, each with its own small waterfall feeding the pool directly below. We rested, ate sandwiches, and swam in one of the bigger pools to cool off. The guides even churned ice cream for us. What a treat.

On the way back, I spotted Rob, the surfer, perched on a twelve-foot-high boulder right in the middle of a large pool. As I watched, he dove in. It looked like fun, so I thought I'd do the same. When I climbed to the top of the boulder, though, I peered down into the pool and saw rocks—large, vertical, submerged rocks that weren't visible at ground level. In fact, I couldn't see any safe spot to dive. Rob pointed to where he dove in, but I didn't like that, either.

You can do it

The problem was the visual distortion in the water. It was hard to determine how close the rocks were to the surface. I decided to go back down the way I had come up, but then discovered that the boulder was more slippery and treacherous climbing down.

How did I get into this mess? I thought. I finally decided that, since I was wearing sneakers, I could use my feet to buffer any contact with the rocks. Plunging into the water feet first, one side of my leg scraped a rock, but it was just a scratch. I was lucky. Lesson learned? Don't try to do what the "jocks" do—especially when they're half your age.

Pulling into camp that night, we were all tired. It had been a long day, and we needed all the sleep we could get. Tomorrow was a special day. Tomorrow we would run Lava.

Lava Falls is considered by many as the fastest navigable rapid in the world, and certainly one of the most dangerous on the Colorado. Thousands of years ago, a volcanic eruption spilled tons of steaming lava into the Colorado River, blocking it. Over eons, the river cut through the lava, forming the narrow gorge that exists today. Rapids can reach as high as fifteen feet, and the water level can drop thirty feet within six seconds.

The next day was hot, in the high nineties. Jeff was our guide. Once again, it was Herb, Barbara, Judy, and me in the raft. Heading down-river, we began to see rock-hard, black lava along the banks. Rounding a bend, Vulcan's Anvil came dramatically into view. It was a solitary pillar of hardened, volcanic lava standing fifteen feet high in the middle of the river—a riveting reminder of where we were, and what we were about to do.

The guides were now quiet and focused. There was no joking or fooling around. They had to scout the overall conditions. How bad would it be today? How fierce were the rapids? How were rafts from other trips on the river doing? Where were the best channels? All this knowledge had to be clear before any of our rafts were committed to the run.

We paddled ashore and the guides, followed by a few of us, climbed to the top of a hill composed entirely of hardened lava. The climb was hot—made even more so by the lava radiating the sun's heat.

Reaching the top, we surveyed the scene below. And what a sight it was. It looked like a devil's cauldron, with rapids smashing into each other from every side. The water was dirty brown and seemed to be boiling.

We saw kayakers from other trips, well-conditioned athletes pitting their skills and flimsy crafts against the raging waters. Only a few made it through without capsizing.

One kayaker who did capsize was underwater for what seemed like minutes. He couldn't surface. His friends rushed to his aid in their kayaks, and almost immediately *they* capsized. Finally, the original kayaker ejected himself from his craft and was carried down river within seconds. His life preserver kept him afloat. He was OK.

The guides reached a decision on their strategy and we returned to the rafts. The plan was to have Ann's raft go first, followed by Jeff (with Herb, Barbara, Judy and me) and Greg. Then Butch and Scott's rafts, carrying the provisions, would go. Chris would bring up the rear. In the event of trouble, two of the most experienced guides would be at each end of the run.

"OK, gang," Greg said, "Let's do it!"

We all watched Ann as she fearlessly attacked the rapid. Although her raft was submerged for most of the two minutes it took to get through, she never lost control or her composure. She was terrific.

Ann Goes For It

Now it was our turn.

Our raft was tethered to shore by two safety lines at the bow and stern. On a command from Jeff, Herb and I released the lines and pulled them into the raft. We were now committed.

Jeff rowed the raft into the river, and we were immediately sucked into the rapids. Their power was overwhelming. They thundered so loud that they sounded like a giant dam bursting. We gripped the safety line that circled the raft and Jeff rowed directly into the maelstrom.

Suddenly, a ten-foot wall of water whacked us and engulfed the raft. Then another wall of water hit us from the other side. And another. All from different directions. I was completely disoriented. I couldn't tell where we were, or where we were going. It was a chaotic combination of massive waves and churning currents. There was simply nothing in my fifty-eight years to equal this experience.

The raft felt like a piece of balsa wood being tossed from crest to crest. Then, horrors, I looked down to see that our raft was now filling with water. Jeff was struggling to maintain control. Suddenly, capsizing was no longer the problem. *Sinking* was.

"Bail!" Jeff yelled at us, "For God's sake, bail!" Bailing, however, meant letting go of our security blanket, the safety line, that we had been holding in a vise-like grip. I wasn't sure I could bail water in this nightmare without falling overboard. (*And wouldn't that be exciting?* I thought). To lessen the possibility, and lower our center of gravity, Herb and I dropped to our knees on the bottom of the raft, bailing the water with plastic buckets. That worked somewhat, but it wasn't pretty. One of us was constantly losing his balance and falling again on the slippery raft floor. We slowly began getting water out, and that helped Jeff regain control of the raft.

Then, suddenly, we were spit out of the angry vortex into calmer waters. We quickly headed for a small beach to secure our raft and wait for the others.

It was over! We had run Lava. We had two immediate emotions: relief and pride. Relief that we had lived; pride that we had done it.

What followed was unbridled euphoria. We broke out beer that the guides had thoughtfully brought along for the celebration. We toasted each other and cheered our companions, who were now doing what we just did. Butch and Scott made it through and joined us at the beach. They were also feeling no pain: they had "graduated." This was their third time, and they were now officially qualified to take passengers in their rafts.

Jeff said, it to no one in particular, "Going through Lava is like doing it for the first time—every time!"

During the last few days of the trip, Judy and I took turns standing tall in the bow of the raft to feel, firsthand, the force of the rapids as they crashed over the raft into us. I also took the oars a few times when we ran some of the less dangerous rapids. It was tougher than I thought to keep the raft upright once we hit white water. I loved it.

On the last day, our take-out—removing the rafts and ourselves from the river—was at Diamond Creek on an Indian reservation. We all helped clean the rafts, deflate them, and load them into one of the most dilapidated buses I had ever seen. It would carry us to the top of the canyon, where our adventure had begun. The heat was oppressive, and we were sweaty, tired, and dirty, and all we wanted at that moment was a cold shower.

Our wayward bus lurched dangerously on the rock-strewn, pot-holed road, edging us up to the south rim. For a brief moment, it looked like we were leaving a war-zone. I held that thought and smiled.

It was the perfect metaphor for our trip.

Bull Elephant

AFRICA

"There's always something new out of Africa."

—*Pliny the Elder (A.D. 23-79)*

Judy and I had always wanted to see Africa, a continent of contrasts, of arid plains and lush pastures, of tropical forests and soaring mountains. But, for us, the main attraction was the animals. We wanted to observe the remaining herds that, at certain seasons, still cover the ground like a carpet. In other places they are few, and in some places, gone forever—annihilated by man.

For me, this urge to see the Dark Continent probably began when I was a kid watching movies of Tarzan, King of the Jungle, whose blood-curdling yell my friends and I would try to emulate. The movies fired our senses with excitement. But Africa was a world away, and, when we were children, the only visit possible had to be imagined.

For years I continued watching movies and TV programs about Africa, but for me, nothing had changed. Africa was always a dream away. After all, who had the time and money for such a trip? Certainly not me, with a demanding job and a growing family.

Things changed when I took early retirement from IBM. Now I had more time and the payoff from some unused vacation days to pay for the trip. Judy and I wrote for catalogs, did some comparison shopping, and decided to go with Abercrombie and Kent (A&K), a reputable, adventure-travel company with years of experience in Africa.

While I was there, I thought I might try to climb Mount Kilimanjaro, one of the goals on my list. A&K came up with a plan that while I was on the mountain, Judy could take a trip into the Ngorongoro Crater in Tanzania and we would meet a week later at a mid-point between both locations.

We opted for a two-week, tented safari that would get us into the bush where the animals were. Our safari was scheduled for the last two weeks in July, with a third week for me to climb Kili, while Judy was visiting the crater.

The preparations were exciting. We got our passports and malaria and tetanus shots. We were constantly on the phone with A&K making last-minute arrangements. They were good folks to work with: patient, professional, and helpful.

On our way to Africa, we stopped for a few days in London to reduce the jet lag. We stayed at Brown's Hotel, where they served the best pot of tea I've ever tasted. Shamelessly, we behaved like the tourists we were, trying to see as many sights as we could squeeze into our three-day schedule. I had considered renting a car, but after watching London traffic for two minutes, I concluded I didn't have that kind of courage.

Our British Airways flight from Heathrow Airport to Nairobi took nine hours, so we were worn out when we arrived in Nairobi, Africa at 6:00 AM. We were met by an A&K representative, who drove us to the historic Norfolk Hotel for an overnight stay. The Norfolk Hotel bar was one of the settings for the Oscar-winning motion picture *Out of Africa,* starring Robert Redford and Meryl Streep. It hasn't changed much since British colonial times, and it was fascinating to be in the actual room where the scenes were shot.

The next day, we lunched at the hotel and explored our surroundings. We were impressed with the size of Nairobi and its cosmopolitan appearance. However, vestiges of its colonized past were everywhere. Tall buildings stood in striking contrast next to small, run-down houses and huts on the outskirts of the city. People got around in a combination of small cars, bicycles, and old buses with people hanging on anywhere they could.

On the day we set off for our safari, Judy and I were picked up by Stanley Nzuki, who would be our driver for the next two weeks. He drove us to the Intercontinental Hotel, where we met our travel companions at an informational meeting hosted by Jim Kanja, who would be the A&K guide for our group. He briefed us on the trip and what we could expect, and he answered questions from the group. Jim, who lives in Nairobi, was soft-spoken with impeccable English. He was tall, with a distinguished closely-cropped black beard. We immediately liked his confidence and sense of humor.

There were sixteen of us would-be adventurers, many from the northeastern part of the United States. Our group included a stock broker from New York City and his eight-year-old son; two gymnastic teachers from Boston; a published author from New York City; a married couple and their two teenage sons from Connecticut; a doctoral candidate from Brooklyn, New York; a pilot from Santa Monica, California, and her girlfriend from New York City; and two young women from Union, New Jersey.

After lunch, we got into three mini-vans, each including six people and a driver. We left Nairobi for our first campsite, Amboseli National Park at the foot of Mount Kilimanjaro. Amboseli is 125 miles south of Nairobi, a three-hour drive over bumpy, dusty roads.

We arrived at five o'clock, tired, sweaty, and dirty. But, after seeing camp, all our complaints were forgotten. It looked like a Hollywood movie set. Large acacia trees surrounded the camp area, which was lined with tents. In front of each tent, on a small table, was a wash pan filled with hot, soapy water. Out of the corner of my eye, I could also see three portable showers begging to be used. A fire made from an eight-foot log crackled, and more wood already was being cut in anticipation of the evening.

I turned my head and saw Kilimanjaro for the first time. The sun was setting, and a pink glow highlighted the mountain's crest. A circular mantle of white clouds hovered under its famous, snowy peak. I was in awe of its beauty and its height (19,342 feet). No wonder local people called it "the home of God." Indeed, the only thing missing from this idyllic scene was Clark Gable or Gregory Peck waving to us as he came back to camp from a successful hunt with a lion slung over his truck.

Our tent was large enough for two cots and a folding bedside table. We dug into our duffel bags, which had been dropped off earlier, for soap and towels so we could take our first shower in the jungle.

We zipped the plastic shower stall closed and released hot water by pulling a chain connected to an overhead bag. There was one shower mishap: Bob, our Ph.D. candidate, pulled the chain too hard, and the entire shower-stall fell over. As if that wasn't enough, the three women waiting in line for their turn began clapping and shouting, "Bravo! Bravo!"

They got an unexpected opportunity to see "the real Bob." Bob was a good sport about the embarrassing moment.

Judy: I was glad Don and I decided on this particular A&K tour. Most of our accommodations were in tents, but we spent some nights in hotels. When tenting, we could be up, in the vans, and out in the bush early in the morning, when the animals were most active. For a change, a night at a hotel or safari club, where we could enjoy a few creature comforts, was welcomed.

The first night, I was relieved to see that the tents were all pitched for us—no wrestling to pitch a tent on this trip. The tents were large and quite comfortable. We stayed at Amboseli several nights, since there was a lot of game in the immediate area.

Then we embarked on a day of travel and animal-viewing. Our "staff" moved our camp completely that day while we stayed at a safari club at night. After days several days in the van, it was nice to luxuriate in a warm tub.

Remarkably, late the next afternoon, we pulled into our new campsite to find the same staff, same tents, etc. The men who traveled with us were the most congenial group, always offering a smile and pleasant word when we spoke to them. They did all the cooking and camp duties, even washing our clothes.

With a woman's curiosity, I went to the dining tent with some of the other gals. The long dining tables were set up with chairs, china, and the works, waiting for us. I asked one of the men who spoke English to give us a quick tour of the kitchen. While we were on the road, they had moved and set up propane-powered Amana freezers and refrigerators, and a huge iron oven and stove, where they cooked roasts and baked pies and cakes for dinner.

Dinner that evening was an American meal of roast turkey, dressing, cranberry sauce, lots of veggies, and tomato soup, followed by a deep-dish rhubarb pie. After dinner, we took our drinks and sat around the fire talking to our new companions. The temperature that night was about sixty degrees Fahrenheit. It was usually in the eighties during the day. We could hear lions roaring in the distance, announcing to all that they were about to hunt.

On the way back to our tent, we saw a tall figure in the shadows. He was dark, lanky, and unmoving. Approaching, we could see that it was a native holding an impressively long spear and shield. He was looking directly at us without any expression. No one else was nearby, and I felt uneasy.

"Jambo!" (Hello), I said. It was one of the few Swahili words I had learned. No response. "Habari?" (How are you?) I asked. Nothing. He didn't move, but his eyes followed our every step as we continued walking to our tent. We would later learn from Jim that he was a full-blooded Masai warrior, hired as a security guard for the camp. That was common practice on safari. His job was to scare curious predators—particularly lions—away from camp. After we turned our lantern out, we could hear many animal sounds, particularly lion and elephants. During the nights to follow, the Masai's presence made sleep seem more secure and appealing.

The next morning, we were up at six o'clock for our first game drive. After breakfast, we piled into our vans to see the early risers among the animals. We hadn't gone more than fifty feet when we saw four wild dogs looking directly at us. They were scrawny, smelly, and, except for their large, sharp teeth, they could have passed for a mangy version of a house pet. However, they were anything but. Wild dogs, especially in a pack, are known to be among the most vicious killers in Africa. It's not uncommon for a pack of these dogs to steal a kill from a pride of lions, such is their ferocity.

Later that morning, we saw seven female lions. Two of them came right up to the side of our van.

Who are these people?

One lioness stared directly at me through a van window that was half open. I could imagine her trying to calculate if she could fit through the opening or not. She couldn't, of course, but just to be sure, I closed the window a few notches.

Kenya has abolished hunting game animals—a law that has benefited both parties. This attracts tourists, and the economy. Wild animals now are generally unafraid of man, and we can get closer to them.

That first day was like driving through an enormous zoo without bars. Animals were everywhere. We saw elephants, giraffes, impalas, monkeys, wart hogs, zebras, and water buffalo. As for the prolific wildebeest, Stanley told us they're about a million strong. I believed him. Just about every predator's favorite meal, the wildebeest cover the plains. And could they run. When a female gave birth, the baby had two or three minutes to be up and running, or its lifespan would be a brief one. Lions, leopards, and cheetahs were always watching the wildebeest for any weaknesses or mistakes of which they could take advantage.

Our van gang was a good group. Sheila, the writer, showed a puckish sense of humor, constantly in play. She was trim and about five-foot-five with dark hair and an inquisitive nature. Bob (of shower stall fame) was earning a doctorate in computer science and using the trip to relax before starting his thesis. He was in his early-thirties and about six feet tall with dark, thinning hair and a quiet manner.

Linda, in her thirties, was a psychotherapist who worked with young people. She was short and perky with boundless energy. Her friend Jean, originally from England, taught gymnastics in a private school outside of Boston. Jean also had energy to burn, and we all enjoyed her English accent. Both ladies were delightful company.

Nick, a New York City stockbroker, had a good sense of humor and used it often. His pronounced New York City accent only enhanced his comments. He and his eight-year old son, Mark, had been planning the African trip for over a year and were very excited. Mark was born with a serious hearing problem that required hearing aids for both ears, a condition that seemed to pose no problem for him. Judy and I were impressed at how routinely, and yet lovingly, father and son handled the disability.

Before going out on a safari, Nick would always remind his son, "Mark, don't forget your ears!" It seemed natural. In fact, I still use some of Nick's reminders with Judy, who has developed a hearing problem of her own.

Our driver, Stanley, was a native African who lived in Nairobi with his wife and five children. Over six feet tall and stocky, Stanley was easygoing and popular with all. We would soon find that he also had an uncanny sense of where animals were located, a valued asset in the bush. He was constantly talking to other van drivers about what they were seeing and where.

On days when we had game drives, we'd usually start out at 6:00 AM, driving into the bush while it was still cool and the animals were active. We'd return to camp at about 9:00 AM for breakfast and then go out again until lunch, after which we'd take a siesta. In the afternoon, we'd go out once more and would roam until sunset. If we were going to a new location the following day, our eight-person staff would break camp and head directly for the new site so they'd be ready for us after we got back from our game drive.

Our next destination was the Aberdare National Park. Since we'd be passing near Nairobi, we were able to lunch at the Carnivore, a well-known restaurant specializing in African game. Antelope, hartebeest, zebra, gerunook, lamb, chicken, and even lion were on the menu. I asked the waiter about lion (not that I was that interested in eating it) and was told that it could only be served if ordered a day ahead so they could pre-cook it. Not exactly a big seller, I figured, and probably not too tender.

After driving 125 miles, we reached the Aberdare Mountains and a country club where we would have dinner and stay overnight. The change from tenting was nice, although, frankly, I liked the tent and the animal sounds that came with it.

At nine thousand feet, the Aberdare Country Club had an old-world charm and enough acreage to accommodate a nine-hole golf course on its mountain. (None of us played because that wasn't why we came to Africa.) Peacocks paraded on the grounds, showing off for anyone who cared to watch them. They seemed almost eager to pose for photos.

After lunch, we transferred to the world-famous Ark, a remarkable building where we would spend the night. Situated in the Aberdare range, this modern Ark, as it were, sits on a seventy-five-hundred-foot spur surrounded by a mountain forest. The Ark can "carry" a maximum of seventy-nine human passengers in double and single rooms. In this version of the ark, the animals stay outside, and the people stay inside.

At dusk, birds, antelope, elephants, cape buffalo, rhinos, and giant forest hogs gathered at the Ark's spotlighted waterhole and salt lick. All three decks of the Ark are all-night observation platforms, and the main viewing lounge is glass-enclosed.

There were vantage points for photographers on all floors, including an eye-level bunker for close-up shots. Until sunrise, animals come to drink water or lick salt. It is one of the few places in the world where animals co-mingle peacefully with each other and people.

We could stay up and view the animals as late as we wanted. If we chose to sleep but wanted to see a particular animal, we would let our guides know, and they would wake us if that animal appeared. After dinner, Judy and I grabbed a few hours sleep and were up at ten o'clock to begin our watch—one that would last until dawn. We spent most of the time on an outside porch that brought us much closer to the animals. I took night shots with slow-speed film and had good results.

Curious Rhinos

As we watched the animals, we saw patterns emerge. Clearly the elephant was boss. When he wanted to drink water or lick salt, the other animals slowly moved out of his way. Even the large, dangerous water buffalo deferred to him. All the animals were generally quiet, almost polite. There was much grunting, but no goring or fighting. It was as if a night-time truce was declared, or as if the Ark were a demilitarized zone where no animal could stomp, kick, or bite.

To cap our vigil—and almost on cue—a lone, magnificent bull elephant came slowly over the horizon at sunrise and went directly to the water hole to drink. It was an appropriate epilogue, we thought, to a memorable night.

Years later, remembering that night, two thoughts would come to mind: The close proximity we shared with the animals, and the sense of respect that prevailed among them. We felt the lack of sleep the next day as we drove 286 miles north to the world-famous Samburu Game Preserve, where we would see a vast variety of wildlife. However, before arriving, we had another adventure.

Stanley was the first in the van to see the elephant herd, eating tree leaves along the road up ahead. One of the elephants was actually on the road, blocking our way. Not wanting to frighten them, Stanley slowed the van. There were eleven adults—all female—and four calves. The adults watched us quietly. Stanley was puttering along in first gear when, suddenly, one of the juveniles broke ranks from the herd and "charged" our van, much like its mother would. Elephant young often imitate their elders in brief displays of ferocity. Usually, we were told, the young elephants stop abruptly and return to the herd.

However, in this instance, the squealing juvenile came very close to us before stopping. This forced Stanley to stop the van for fear of hitting him. When the mother saw her calf so close to the van, she got nervous and started toward us. Knowing elephants as he did, Stanley didn't like what was developing and knew we should get out of there, pronto! The juvenile saw his upset mother coming toward him. Probably thinking that she was also going to attack the van, he began to squeal all the more and wave his miniature trunk.

In that moment, Stanley gunned the motor and did an end-run around the whole herd by driving the van off the road into the tall grass and back up on the road again. The juvenile, now tired of the game, stopped. However, his mother didn't. She was still ticked off and continued to pursue us. Judy and I were in the back of the van, looking through the rear window at this huge female elephant chasing us. For a few seconds it was tense—especially when Stanley had trouble shifting into high gear and the elephant was getting ever closer. But once the van was in third-gear, we left her swinging her trunk at us with unmistakable anger.

We reached camp in Samburu in time for lunch, after which we left on a game drive through this semi-arid country. We saw Grevy zebras, reticulated giraffes, and graceful, long-necked gerenuks, antelopes that can reach the tallest branches by standing straight up on their hind legs. That night after dinner, we fell into our cots early. It had been a long day. A great day.

We had a second day of game drives in Samburu, with the Uase Nyiro River and the Ololokwe Mountains providing a striking backdrop. We saw more elephants, some buffalo, and our first moving troop of about thirty baboons. We were close to the baboons as they passed by, and they weren't the least bothered by our presence.

We watched the babies hang nervously on their mothers' bodies, wherever they could grab hold. Some rode on their mothers' backs, which required a degree of balance that most of them didn't have. Others clung to their mothers' underbellies with varying degrees of success. If they fell off, the mothers kept right on going, and the babies had to catch up and jump back to their original positions, top or bottom.

Shortly after we saw the baboons, another driver yelled to Stanley that he had seen a male leopard. The leopard had just made a kill a mile south of us. We jumped into the van and headed that way. Leopard sightings are rare, so we were excited. After a ten-minute drive, we stared at the clump of bushes where the leopard allegedly was. Within minutes, another van full of people pulled up. Like us, they had their cameras at the ready and were eager to see Africa's most elusive cat.

Suddenly the leopard exploded out of the bushes about ten feet in front of us. Carrying a dead impala in its mouth, the leopard effortlessly scaled a large tamarind tree. Within seconds, he reached a large branch and positioned his kill in a notch of the tree. The impala was now completely out of sight, and we had to look hard to even see the leopard.

Stanley learned that the female leopard was also nearby, so he quickly circled the van around a grove of trees. There, sunning herself on a big log, sat the female—regal, beautiful, and indifferent. We all began taking pictures as fast as our shutters would permit. Then Judy spotted the leopard's two cubs partially hidden under a big log. We moved closer, only twenty feet from her. She didn't run as leopards usually do. She seemed unafraid and content to lie in the sun. I didn't see her cubs because I was too busy taking photos of the mother—photos that turned out to be the best of the trip.

Leopardess basking in sun (2 cubs under tree stump)

Our experience with the leopards had a postscript. When we were maneuvering our van for a better look at the first leopard, Sheila noticed that one woman in the other van (not A&K) was not even looking at the leopard but was filing her fingernails. The woman's hair was rolled up in goofy-looking pink curlers (probably preparing for dinner that night) and she was completely focused on her nails—ignoring one of Africa's most spectacular animals.

In the mid-eighties, there was a humorous commercial on television about Grey Poupon mustard. It showed a Rolls Royce automobile with an obvious aristocrat in the back seat driving up beside another Rolls Royce with yet another aristocrat in the backseat. In a bored voice, the first aristocrat asked the second, "I say, would you by chance have any Grey Poupon?"

The woman doing her nails reminded Sheila of that commercial and an idea surfaced. She turned to Stanley.

"Stanley, would it be too much trouble to move our van next to that van so I can talk to the lady in curlers?" Obligingly, Stanley moved the van so that the windows lined up. The woman was still doing her nails. Sheila opened her window and in a loud but bored voice asked the woman, "I say, would you by chance have any Grey Poupon?"

The woman stared at Sheila as if she were from another planet. She didn't say a word. She didn't blink. She just stared, her nail file frozen in the air. For her, the scene didn't compute. It was obvious she had never encountered anyone like Sheila.

As our van pulled away, we could see that the lady in curlers had recovered and was back to her nails, as if nothing ever happened. We could only imagine her dinner conversation that night.

After many days in the bush, our next stop was a rewarding change of pace. We were to spend a day and night at the Mount Kenya Safari Club, a beautiful resort made famous by the late Bill Holden, an Oscar-winning Hollywood actor. Holden and his long-time companion, actress Stephanie Powers, founded the William Holden Wildlife Foundation, which is headquartered at the club. When we were there, the foundation was active with endangered animal breeding programs and other educational projects.

Seeing Mount Kenya (17,058 feet) and its glaciers for the first time is impressive. Sitting practically on the equator, the mountain is a perfect backdrop for the club's beautiful buildings, manicured grounds, large swimming pool, and Marabou storks that stroll freely on the property. These storks are large, white birds with long, stout bills and spindly legs. Their wings are greenish gray, and they have large pouches beneath their bills. They eat smaller birds, small mammals, and lizards.

More than fifty storks were sitting or walking around the grounds with unconcealed indifference, almost a sense of impunity. Some were on rooftops sitting in nests they made atop unused chimneys. Seeing them there reminded us of the old fables about storks delivering babies.

Judy and I had such a large, elegant room for the night that we thought there might be some mistake. Jim Kanja, our guide who helped us with our luggage, told us that this was Bill Holden's room when he came to Africa, but that seemed hard to believe. True or not, it made for a good story.

As Judy and I unpacked, we heard loud drumming below our windows. Looking outside, we saw nine or ten native dancers in ceremonial dress dancing on the grass to the drums and their own infectious rhythm. They were young, well-muscled men who danced vigorously to a tribal chant. Many of us went outside with cameras to record the scene. The dancers never stopped to pose for pictures or talk to any of us. They were there to dance, and when they finished, they left as quickly as they had come.

Another highlight was the formal dinner that evening in the Safari Club Grill-Room, which was out of character with everything we had been doing in the jungle. Dinner jackets and ties were required for the men and dresses for the ladies, so it was a bit difficult to recognize our companions.

Everyone looked so civilized that we weren't always sure who was who. There were many toasts, most of them humorous, including a special one for our guide, Jim, whose wife had delivered a baby son that very morning. It was a fun evening, tastefully done, and it made our small group even tighter than it had been.

The next morning, we drove 130 miles to Lake Navaisha, where we would see hippos up close and personal. Stanley also pointed out the small bungalow where Joy Adamson, author of *Born Free*, lived before her death in 1980.

We had lunch along the shores of Lake Nakuru, famous for the flamingos (more than two million by some estimates) that feed and breed in the lake. When the flamingos took flight, the sky turned pink.

Judy and I saw our first hyena along the lakeshore (probably looking for a flamingo dinner). Dog-like in appearance, the hyena is recognizable by its sloping, streamlined back. We got out of the van for a closer look, and the hyena gave us a malevolent, toothy grin.

Waterbuck haunt the environs of Lake Naivasha, along with wiry colobus monkeys that we saw leaping from tree to tree. Fish eagles, strikingly handsome birds, nest in trees around the lake. They reminded us of our own American bald eagle. They were just as beautiful, with a similar predatory look.

Hippos, despite their goofy appearance, are very dangerous and not to be fooled with. They are always territorial and can be very aggressive. They are also responsible for more deaths to humans than any other African mammal. It's well known in Africa that hippos can outrun a man on a beach or any flat stretch of ground.

Five of us—Linda, Jean, Judy, me, and Norman, our native pilot—went out on the lake in a small outboard motor boat. When the hippos saw us, they immediately erupted into a chorus of watery grunts. They showed their annoyance by tossing their huge heads in a threatening fashion and retreated to deeper water. There were several herds. Some were in the lake, others basking on shore. Norman said that as long as the hippos have access to deep water, they usually don't feel threatened. But whenever our boat got too close, the hippos grunted and twitched their ears while eyeing us warily.

I was sitting in the stern of the boat a scant fifteen feet away from a large hippo when I noticed that he was staring at me and hardly moving. It was as if he knew where his turf began and how close we were to it. Just his head and his pink-tinged back were out of the water. Hippos have glands that secrete a red fluid that drips like lacquer on their backs to protect them from the sun and dehydration. As we sat there with the motor off, I felt vulnerable and wondered, *If that hippo decided to attack this boat, would we have enough time to turn the motor back on and get out of here?* I did not think so.

The next morning, we left Lake Naivasha and headed 190 miles north into Serengeti National Park to the Masa Mara, the most game-filled area in Africa. This is where we would spend our last two days on safari. Populating the Masa Mara are large herds of impala, buffalo, giraffe, zebra, gazelles, and the reclusive topi, an antelope with grey flanks. These are annually reinforced by the thundering legions of wildebeest and all of their opportunistic predators: lions, cheetah, hyena, leopard, water buffalo, and jackals.

On a well-traveled part of the road to the Masai Mara, we stopped to eat at a small teahouse. Normally, all the water we drank in camps was boiled first, and at restaurants on the road, we would get boiled water from the bar. The system worked well, and no one had gotten sick. But on that hot day, Judy ordered iced tea with her meal. Later, Jim came by while we were eating and noticed the ice in Judy's tea. He said, "Don't drink any more until I find out if the water for the ice was boiled."

Jim came back and sure enough, it had not. Even though Judy drank only a small amount, she still developed cramps, diarrhea, and other flu-like symptoms that afternoon. However, probably because Jim had caught the problem early, she was spared serious illness.

Because Judy felt lousy, she couldn't visit the Masai village we had planned to see that afternoon. I took the small gifts we had bought earlier for the Masai children and told her I'd see that they got them.

The village was a small cluster of mud huts with thatched roofs. It was populated mostly by women, children, and elders because the men were away herding cattle or hunting. We had been briefed by A&K in how to be respectful of Masai customs, and I think we all were.

For about twenty minutes, we walked around the village and later participated in a simple ceremony of greeting. When the tribal members lined up in the center of the *boma (*compound), we walked single file down the line of fifteen or twenty Masai tribal members to say j*ambo* (hello), to their *karibu (*welcome). Our gifts for the children included ballpoint pens, combs, and chewing gum. The villagers were very appreciative and said *assante* (thank you).

Even though the Masai were hospitable, I felt I was intruding. Some of our group went inside the huts, entering on their hands and knees to get through the low entrance. I chose not to intrude but was told later that the only possessions inside the limited space were mats to sleep on and bowls and utensils for cooking. For me, the visit was sobering. It's one thing to see a movie clip of such living conditions but quite another to experience it first hand. The visit highlighted for me the enormous inequities in the world and how much needs to be done to achieve simple, basic needs for millions of people.

The Masa Mara is the northern extension of the Serengeti and the richest year-round game land in Africa. In this area of teeming wildlife, Stanley told us we would be observing lions that day and seeing the precision they bring to the hunt. If we were lucky, Stanley said, we might see a lion pride hunting for wildebeest. We drove to high ground overlooking the Mara River, wending its way through the savanna. We parked near an area frequented by lions.

It wasn't long before three lions—two females and a young male—came over to our van, sniffed it, and looked directly at us. There's something unsettling about looking at three hungry lions eye to eye—van or no van. Soon, almost on cue, they left in single file and headed for the river. As we watched, each of them took positions along the high ground above the river. They were about fifty yards from each other. From our position, we could see little of the shallow section of the Mara River, where the wildebeest would soon be crossing.

Stanley told us he would get us as close as possible, and yet not so close as to disturb the lions. We then drove quietly to another location, lower than the first, where we could see two lions about fifty feet away from each other.

They were waiting, and so were we.

Then we heard the wildebeest approaching. We couldn't see them, but we could hear a constant roar of grunting confusion. Stanley, now excited himself, described to us what he thought was happening.

"Lions wait. And watch. And when wildebeest start to fall over each other, trying to get across river, the lions attack," Stanley said. "Five or six lions, mostly females. It's over quickly."

That evening in camp, the lion attack was the major topic of conversation. And while we didn't see the actual attack for safety reasons, we had a good idea of what happened. We could hear the wildebeest and the lions. Seeing the lions position themselves in anticipation of the attack—along with Stanley's whispered description of what happens in such attacks—was something that we hadn't expected.

After the day's excitement, most of us were quiet and reflective, knowing that our trip was over. It reminded me of a comment that Karen Blixen, who wrote *Out Of Africa,* once made about her beloved Kenya home: "Here I am, where I ought to be."

Now Judy and I knew why she felt that way.

BALLOONING

Flying in a hot air balloon had always struck me as a unique experience. When Judy and I were planning our African safari, we discovered that for an extra $230 each, we could go ballooning over the jungle. We signed on.

Our adventure began at 4:00 AM, deep in Africa's Masa Mara Game Preserve, when the guides awakened us in our tents and told us to get dressed. It was very dark and surprisingly chilly. We could see flashlights bobbing around in other tents and hear the voices of the seven other people who signed up for ballooning as they searched for their shoes, warm sweaters, eyeglasses.

Soon we were in our vans, groggily heading to the patch of open field where our jungle flight would begin at early dawn. According to our driver, Jason, the balloons we'd be using were large.

"Biggest in the world," he said quietly.

Before take off

The road was rocky and jolted us completely awake. Soon we were alert and beginning to anticipate our adventure. After an hour of driving, we finally reached our destination. It was still dark with a small glow of sunrise on the horizon.

Then we saw the balloons. *My God*, I thought. *Jason was right. They're enormous!* There were three of them, lined up next to each other, and a number of people were working on them. We spilled out of the van for a closer look.

As we watched the blowers and burners at work, I tried to recall from high school chemistry the basic laws that govern ballooning. Air expands when heated, making the heated air (or gas) inside a balloon less dense—or lighter—than the surrounding air. The difference in density makes the balloon rise. Heat for the hot air comes from burning propane, a safe and inexpensive gas. The burner produces a flame that reaches up into the open tube in the balloon.

To inflate a hot-air balloon, the pilot spreads the balloon on the ground so the top of the bag lies downwind from the basket. The pilot lays the basket down sideways, facing the balloon, and attaches the basket to the bottom of the balloon. A large fan then blows air into the mouth of the balloon. When it's about half-inflated, the pilot starts the burner. As the air is heated, the balloon begins to slowly rise, pulling the basket upright. The balloon then hangs over the burner and basket in a vertical position.

A free-floating balloon travels in whichever direction the wind blows. A pilot can control only the vertical movement of a manned balloon. He cannot steer it. However, the pilot can control the course of a balloon flight to some degree by rising or descending to find a wind that's blowing in the desired direction.

We watched the three balloons in varying stages of readiness. Two were lying on the ground. A large fan was blowing air into one of them, while air for the second, half-inflated balloon was being heated. The third balloon was already in its vertical position and ready to go. It looked about as high as a three-story department store. We could see intermittent bursts of flame as the propane burner kept the balloon's air heated.

When the first balloon took off, it was something to see. This massive red and blue balloon with ten people (some from other groups) in its basket rose gracefully into the still, dark sky. Like a metronome, the cadence of its fiery retorts could be heard from its propane burner as we watched from the ground.

Within minutes, the second balloon—equally colorful—began its graceful ascent in slow pursuit of the first. We watched them floating silently toward an emerging sunrise. Now it was our turn. Our balloon was in the vertical position, and our gang of eight was anxious to board. We met our pilot, Duncan, an Australian. Tall, with rugged good looks, Duncan had a moustache that reminded me of John Cleese of Monty Python fame.

After brief introductions, Duncan said, "Jolly good. Time to go. Shall we hop in the basket?"

We clambered in. The basket was made of woven wicker, a strong, lightweight material that can absorb shocks in rough landings, and was large enough to accommodate as many as twelve people.

Duncan was congenial and answered our questions while working. He operated the burner that was fixed to a metal platform just above the basket and directly below the bag's mouth. During one of Duncan's monologues, he casually told us that he was missing a leg. We were surprised, since most of us had never been on a balloon trip with a one-legged pilot. However, it didn't appear to hinder his operation of the balloon or, for that matter, his on-going chatter. He moved around on his artificial leg so adroitly we soon forgot about it.

We were now rising above the tree line, a dramatic sensation. Our eyes were trying to absorb a palette of images: the landscape of course, and the animals that were now running crazily at every bark of the burner. For Judy and me, one of the most stunning sights was watching the two balloons ahead of us, silhouetted against a brilliant sunrise.

At about one hundred feet we looked below and saw, of all things, a swimming pool, and a man in bathing trunks looking up at us—as if *we* were the oddity. The scene didn't compute. What was a swimming pool doing in the middle of the jungle? we asked Duncan.

"That's a safari club for tourists who sleep over, like yourselves," Duncan said. "He's probably a guest."

The explanation made sense, but the incongruity of the scene did not.

It was about seven o'clock, and most of the animals were active. We saw zebra, impalas and other antelopes, as well as an elephant. The ubiquitous wildebeest went "bonkers every time the burner fired. As we rose higher, there was less noise to bother the animals, and they panicked less.

At two hundred feet, the scene below seemed like a micro-cosm of Africa. We saw herds of antelope in one part of the Masa Mara—oblivious to a herd of zebra a half mile away. Mini-dramas played out below. One zebra walked unwittingly on a path that led to an elephant eating tree leaves. We knew they would meet and wondered what would happen. We watched, fascinated. Predict-ably, the zebra spotted the elephant and made a quick right-turn to another trail. No fool, that zebra.

"We're getting close to the Tanzanian border," Duncan announced, "and that's off-limits for us. If we had to land there, Tanzanian authorities would confiscate the balloon. So, I'm going higher to catch some northerly winds that will move us off this course."

Soon we were at 250 feet, and the scene below was even more miniscule. It was about then it happened.

Blam!

We heard a loud report, like a rifle shot. Our basket felt as though it hit something, and seemed to stop in flight. We were all jostled and thrown against each other. Two women fell to the bas-ket floor. I shouted to no one in particular, "What the hell was that?"

Then, to our horror, the balloon began to descend precipi-tously.

"Wind shear!! I do think we've hit wind shear!" Duncan yelled at us, almost light-heartedly, as if it were a common occurrence. In all my years of business travel for IBM, I had never experienced wind shear, which is a sudden change of wind speed or direction over a short distance and can be very dangerous. Don Estridge, an IBM executive considered the father of the IBM personal com-puter, died in a fatal airline accident caused by wind shear over Dallas, Texas. All passengers on the plane were killed.

We were still descending much too fast. Duncan had turned the burner on full to heat more air and slow our descent. None of us passengers really understood what was happening. Finally the balloon began to drop more slowly. At about eighty feet from the ground, Duncan shouted, "Hold on to the basket, bend your knees, and hold on tight! This could be a bumpy landing."

Talk about understatement. We hit the ground very hard. Four people fell inside our basket, amid much yelling and confusion. Judy and I looked at each other. We were OK. As we started to help those on the basket floor, our second balloon ride of the day—a horizontal one—began.

Because of its sudden descent, the balloon was still partially inflated and was now literally being blown across the African landscape. The only thing preventing the balloon from becoming airborne again was the collective weight of the basket, with us in it.

At that point, the basket was no longer upright but diagonal to the ground. The yelling and confusion continued.

"Don't panic! Don't panic!" Duncan shouted. (As if we had a choice.)

There was little we could do as long as the partially inflated balloon was being bounced by the wind across the flat grassland.

Then, I saw it about fifty yards ahead—a large, up-ended tree trunk. *We're going to hit it!* I thought.

And we did. On collision, the exposed roots of the tree functioned like oversized meat hooks. The roots caught the basket and stopped it.

Balloon caught on tree stump

Our ride from hell was over. In those first few seconds, the silence was palpable. Then, some of the passengers began to groan.

"You okay?" someone asked.

"Yeah, I think so," a woman answered.

"What stopped us?" someone wondered.

"What was that all about?"

"I banged my chin on the basket. It's bleeding," a woman moaned.

Incredibly, no one was seriously hurt. We were all bounced around a bit, but most of us thought that a small price, considering what could have happened.

The original plan for concluding our balloon ride called for a breakfast at a landing site a mile from where we were now. However, once Duncan called A&K on his portable telephone to report our crash, the company did the right thing and brought the champagne breakfast to us.

Later, as we were eating, Judy looked over at me. She was holding a glass of champagne and looked very serious. She held up her glass—as if to toast—paused a moment and said: "And you wanted a little adventure in our lives"

CLIMBING MOUNT KILIMANJARO

I had longed for years to climb Mount Kilimanjaro, Africa's highest mountain at 19,340 feet. It was a dream fueled by Ernest Hemingway's stories about the fabled peak.

What to do? Give it a try, of course. Two, actually.

I failed on my first attempt and decided to try again. In the process, I hiked into the clouds with a one-legged man, met a former president of the United States, and discovered that, as a codger of sixty, I could still push myself further and higher than I believed possible.

I first tried to climb the mountain, which rises above the jungles of Tanzania in east Africa, in 1987. I was fifty-nine, just retired from my job at IBM and in relatively good shape. Or so I thought. To reach Kilimanjaro's summit, you don't need ropes, pitons, or pick-axes. But you do need endurance to hike steadily into air that becomes increasingly thin. It was this lack of oxygen that did me in, and at somewhat more than three miles above sea level, I could go no farther.

In 1988, I decided to try again, and an early retirement check made a second trip possible. Even so, with expenses projected at close to five thousand dollars, we decided that since we had been on safari last year, Judy would sit this one out. Time was a major consideration. Because of my age, if I were to have any chance of reaching Kili's summit, I couldn't wait too long. I was already getting a bit old for the hike, in some doctors' opinions, and I wanted to take advantage of the effort and knowledge from my first attempt.

Before my first attempt, I had passed a complete physical exam and thought I could handle climbing Kilimanjaro. In retrospect, this was naive. Except for infrequent workouts at a health club, I was unprepared for the mountain. Over age fifty, the body's ability to deliver oxygen to cells is compromised by the normal aging process. Blood vessels narrow, and there's always the danger of edema—a combination of higher blood pressure and lower oxygen content. Edema causes capillaries to fill the lungs with fluid (pulmonary edema) or the brain (cerebral edema).

If that happens, the only solution is to get down to a lower altitude as fast as you can. Or die.

In that first climb, I experienced a frightening light-headedness halfway up the summit that led to hallucinations. That, plus total exhaustion, made my decision to go down an easy one.

When I decided to try again the following year, I exercised for nine months at the same health club, but this time I also hiked outside on tough mountains near our home. I took another physical, including stress tests (striding uphill on a treadmill). I could see improvement in my strength and endurance. Not exactly Marathon Man, but more fit—and wiser. However, I was also a year older.

As our van pulled up to the Kibo Hotel at the base of the mountain, I wondered if this second attempt would be different. Lekule, my young lead guide from a year ago, was waiting in the hotel courtyard with a wide grin.

"Karibu, Papa, karibu!" he said, using the Swahili word for hello. "Good to see you again. This time we go to top, OK?" I was called "Papa" by Lekule and many of the porters, some of whom I didn't even know. They seemed to have their own network, knowing just about everyone who was on the mountain at any given time.

Lekule, in his mid-twenties, stood about five and a half feet tall and was wiry and strong for his 150-pound frame. His number one porter was his cousin, Millard, who was named for the thirteenth U.S. president, Millard Fillmore. Millard was about thirty and served as an elder advisor to Lekule, helping solve the many problems and disputes that can occur on a climb.

From left, Millard, Lekule, and Stevie

Filling out our five-man team were three other porters, including fifteen-year-old Stevie (a relative of Millard), the youngest of the group. Stevie's sunny disposition and willingness to work would make him a valued member of the climb.

There was a lot to carry, including gear, clothing, food, and firewood for cooking. (The Tanzanian Park Department forbids cutting trees for firewood on the mountain.) I was also taking a case of bottled water this time, not wishing to test my luck on the few mountain springs whose water was just "OK" to drink.

We would start my second climb early in the morning. Three camps were involved: Mandara, at nine thousand feet; Horombo, at twelve thousand feet; and Kibo, at 15,500 feet. From Kibo, we would make the final ascent to the summit. I added an extra day at Horombo to acclimatize to the altitude, so for me the climb would be six days, not five as it had been the year before.

According to Tanzanian officials, you've officially climbed Mount Kilimanjaro if you reach Gilman's Point at 18,600 feet. This rim overlooks the extinct volcano that crowns the mountain with its famous mantle of frozen snow. Seven hundred and forty feet higher is Uhuru Peak, which, at 19,340 feet, is actually the highest point on the mountain. However, many climbers who make it to the top stop at Gilman's. My plan was to do the same. There were thirty-six climbers starting out with me that cool August morning. Most were from Germany, Italy, France, and Switzerland; some were from England and Japan. Eight of us were from the United States. I was impressed by everyone's athletic appearance. They were all trim and clean-cut, mostly in their twenties and thirties. A few were in their forties and fifties. At sixty, I was the oldest.

The morning was crisp, about fifty degrees Fahrenheit. I was excited but a little apprehensive. I had butterflies before the big game. Lekule, wearing a jaunty Australian bush hat, and Millard and the porters were all in good spirits as we loaded our gear into the van that would take us to the park gate and the start of our journey. We drove through Marangu Village, past banana trees and wide-eyed children, up a steep road to the gate where we would begin our climb.

It usually takes four hours to cover the six or so miles to Mandara (nine thousand feet), where we would spend our first night. A broad forest trail soon narrowed to a dense semi-tropical rain forest. Great trees, twisted into many shapes, formed a dense canopy, with moss and lichen dropping from their branches.

Semi-tropic rain forest near Mandara

I drank fluids often, even when I wasn't thirsty, and ate a trail mix rich in carbohydrates and protein to helped prevent the dehydration and fatigue that plagued me a year earlier. And perhaps the best climbing advice Lekule gave me was: "Pole, Pole" (pronounced POLey), Swahili for slowly.

I learned from our guides that sometimes there are antelope, buffalo, and rhino deep in the forests of Kilimanjaro, but they are rarely seen. The occasional leopard, which hunts the antelope, is even more elusive. It was probably such a leopard that was found frozen at the summit in 1926, later inspiring Hemingway's *The Snows of Kilimanjaro.*

Mandara at base of Kilimanjaro

Sighting Mandara, at the base of Kilimanjaro, I felt better than I did last year at this time. At my pace, the climb took me more hours than anyone else, but I wasn't worried about time or being the last to arrive. Just getting there was my goal.

The cluster of A-frame huts at Mandara was scattered around a central dining hut that is larger than the other buildings. Each hut contained two rooms, and four bunks to a room. Mandara offered the first clear view over the hilly forest to the plains below. As we finished dinner, clouds just below us, crowned by a beautiful sunset, enveloped the camp. The evening meal, prepared by the porters, was basic but tasty: meat, potatoes, vegetables, bananas for desert and the ubiquitous English tea.

I met a young couple from London, Tony and Dorothy James, and we shared dinner. I also met Dr. Donald Gaxti, a college president from Missouri who, amazingly, was climbing with one leg. His other limb was artificial but didn't seem to slow him a bit.

It was Dr. Gaxti who first informed me that we might have a problem. He learned that no one would be allowed to go to Horombo the next morning because former president Jimmy Carter and his party would be there. The Secret Service was concerned for the president's safety because of increased terrorism in some parts of Africa. The Secret Service had made arrangements with the Tanzanian Park Department to keep all climbers at the nine thousand foot level (Mandara) until the Carter party left Horombo (twelve thousand feet). We were told that any climbers found near Horombo would be sent back.

Losing an extra day would torpedo my schedule. I'd have to rearrange my remaining days just to make the return flight home. I was less than thrilled with the news.

Weeks before leaving for Africa, I had read in the paper that the former president and his family planned to climb the mountain. While I'd been struck by the coincidence, I hadn't thought much about it until I arrived at Kibo Hotel and saw a big welcome sign for Carter. I was told by J. La Brosse, the hotel manager (and, allegedly, a former member of the French Foreign Legion), that the Carter party was ahead of us and would be coming down from the summit as I was heading up.

He said at the time that climbers might be held up overnight because of the presidential party, but it wasn't definite. I asked him to please give the Secret Service my name, establish that I was an American, and tell them when I was due to arrive at Horombo. He said he would.

Now here we were at Mandara, with no telephone communication, being told that we couldn't climb tomorrow morning. Most climbers were upset with the news, but few talked about defying the ban.

I huddled with Dr. Gaxti, discussing the idea of taking our chances and climbing anyway. "We're Americans," I said. "You're a one-legged college president from Missouri, and I'm a sixty-year-old retired IBMer from New Jersey. What can they do to us?"

Dr. Gaxti peered at me for a moment, smiled and said blandly, "Shoot us."

Without telling anyone except the porters who would come with us, we decided to leave early in the morning.

The way to Horombo

The eight-mile hike to the Horombo usually took four hours. At my pace, I figured six to seven at the very least. After a brilliant sunrise and hearty breakfast, we were off, plunging immediately into rain forest. The ground was muddy and steep. We grabbed on to large roots and vines to pull ourselves up the slope. Climbing was slippery and strenuous, and soon our clothes were soaked by the high humidity.

It was impressive how porters could balance thirty or forty pound loads on their heads while climbing such difficult terrain. Many guides climb Kilimanjaro two and three times a month, with each roundtrip climb lasting about five days. Even though guides are acclimatized to the altitude, it's still a punishing schedule. All but the heartiest need days off between climbs.

Most porters in their twenties and thirties have no problems with the mountain. However, I did see some as young as eleven and twelve struggling with their loads, and a few as old as sixty-five stooped over by theirs. I came across one elderly porter on the trail who was sitting down looking at his bleeding heel. A metal clip had broken on his sandal and was digging into the skin. With the aid of a rock, I was able to bang the clip back close to its original shape and apply a large Band-Aid to his bruise.

"Asante" (thank you), he said, giving me a big smile as he got back on the trail. I suspect he would have kept on going until he could go no farther, such was his desire to continue with a job he probably had been doing for decades.

After an hour, the landscape began to change into open, rolling moorland dotted with thirty-foot-tall heather trees. Violets and other delicate wildflowers filled the spaces between great clumps of grass. Suddenly, I saw Kilimanjaro's peak. It was nestled in clouds that were moving just slowly enough to confuse the viewer as to what was cloud and what was mountain. Just as quickly as it appeared, the great skullcap of snow was gone, enveloped again by clouds. But it was there. I saw it.

People were now coming down the trail with their porters running ahead, eager to finish their journey and collect their pay. Even as I breathed heavily in the thin air, I saw a number of porters smoking cigarettes. Like our group, the descending climbers represented many nationalities. They were coming down from Kibo hut, the highest on the mountain. It was hard to tell from their expressions if they had made the summit or not. Lekule had told me earlier, "Unless they're smiling, don't ask!"

Lekule also told me, "Sometimes there's lion near Horombo"—something I hadn't realized.

"Three years ago," he said, "lioness follow porter back to camp. She run off when she see other porters near fire." I promised myself I'd not stray from camp. Especially at night.

At eleven thousand feet, the landscape became rocky. My breathing was labored. I concentrated on climbing slowly, even though I seemed to have more energy than a year ago. I caught up with Dr. Gaxti, who hadn't stopped for lunch and was hiking, like the wise tortoise, at his slow but steady pace. He used two walking sticks with synchronized efficiency.

At this level, we saw magnificent giant groundsel and lobelia plants that have adapted to the hostile environment, growing to a height of ten to fifteen feet. At first sight, they looked like the large cactus plants found in the southwestern United States.

Nearing Horombo, I began to worry. I could see three men in the distance working along the camp's perimeter. *Uh, oh, Secret Service*, I thought. They were working on what looked like a portable transmitter. They were completely engrossed in their work. As we came closer, I could see no way to slip by them. About then, I thought it a good idea to stay close to Dr. Gaxti. Surely, they wouldn't send a one-legged man all the way down to Mandara, I thought. And if they didn't send him down, maybe they wouldn't send me. Moments before we would have to pass them, I decided to take the initiative.

"Is it working yet?" I asked, pointing at the transmitter. Surprised, all three men rose as one and looked at us.

"Who are you?" one asked. Thinking that Dr. Gaxtie was our strongest card, I whispered to him, "Tell 'em, Don!" Without missing a beat, Gaxtie said in a stentorian voice, "I'm Dr. Donald Gaxtie, President of North Central Missouri College." For them, the scene didn't compute, and, for a moment, they were speechless. Not to lose the advantage, Dr. Gaxtie quickly added, "Beautiful view, what?" The normalcy of the question must have conveyed some degree of assurance because they slowly replied, "Yes, it is. It sure is."

We didn't slow our pace but kept walking and talking with great purpose, as if heading for an important meeting. We hadn't a clue as to where we were going, but our pace suggested otherwise. After a few moments, they lost interest and went back to their work. We had made it. We now had our pick of the empty huts, since we were the only ones there besides the Carter people. We were very tired, so we agreed to rest and meet later for dinner.

I was alone, heading for one of the huts, when I saw him. The former president was shaving. There was no one else around. I was about ten yards away, and I could either keep going or go over and say hello. After all, when would such an opportunity come again? I turned and walked directly toward him. He looked up. He was somewhat rumpled and looked tired.

"Hello, Mr. President," I said, "I'm Don Mac Isaac from New Jersey. How did you do this morning?"

He began talking as if I were a longtime friend.

"Well, I finally made it to Gilman's Point," he said, "but it was hard. Harder than I thought." Flashing his famous toothy smile, he said, "I'm bushed." Then, looking at me, he asked, "Are you going up tomorrow?"

"The day after," I replied, explaining that I wanted an extra day at Horombo to acclimatize after my problems of last year.

He seemed impressed that I would try again. "Well, good for you," he said, "I don't think I'd want to do this climb again."

Dinner that evening was special, enjoyed by a happy Carter entourage of close to forty people. Most of them were porters. The rest were family: the former president; his wife, Rosalynn; their son, Chip; Chip's wife and children, other relatives, and Secret Service agents. Dr. Gaxti and I were the only outsiders.

I ended up sitting between two Secret Service agents. They talked about the problems of protecting an ex-president who likes to jog, camp out, and climb tall mountains in Africa.

"Very stressful," they said. Both of them were just recovering from altitude sickness. Even though they were thirty years younger than the former president, they said they were unable to keep up with him on his way to the top.

Since this was to be the last dinner of their trip, the lead guide gently tapped a glass with his spoon for attention and proceeded to give a warm, impromptu talk. He thanked President Carter and his family for coming to Tanzania and honoring the country. The guide praised their accomplishment (Jimmy made it to Gilman's

Point, and Rosalynn climbed to Hans Meyer Cave.) and, on behalf of his porters, told the Carters how enjoyable it was for him and the porters to climb with the former president. He praised the work that Mr. Carter was doing to help third-world nations.

"Such dedication commands the respect of all nations and good people," the guide said.

The former president graciously thanked him and his staff for helping make possible an exciting and unforgettable trip for the Carter party.

The next morning, Carter and his party were up early for their long descent to the park gate. The Carters also had agreed to pose for a few photos.

Dr. Gaxtie had asked me earlier if I'd take some pictures of the Carters with his camera, since it took a while to prepare his prosthesis in the morning. With two cameras strung around my neck, I joined the others and began taking pictures of the Carter family for Dr. Gaxtie and myself. Then I saw one of the Secret Service men I had dinner with the night before coming toward me.

"Hey Don, want a picture with Jimmy?" he asked.

"Sure," I said. "That would be nice!"

Moments later, I saw my new friend walking toward me, with not only President Carter, but Mrs. Carter as well.

"Well, hello again!" the former president said with a big smile.

Before I could respond, he turned to Rosalyn and said, "He was here last year, but didn't make it to the top. So he's trying again."

With that, Mrs. Carter came over to me and said, "Well, good for you, I think that's great! And I bet you'll make it this time!" She stood beside me and motioned to her husband to stand on my other side.

From left, former President Jimmy Carter, Don and Rosalyn Carter

As my Secret Service friend fired off a few shots with my camera, I couldn't help thinking, unless one of these pictures comes out, nobody will believe this.

That morning started my extra day to adjust to the altitude. I took short walks around the site but mostly took it easy. By midday, all huts were filled with climbers coming up from Mandara. Because of the climbing ban, there were more people than bunks that night. Many had to sleep on hut floors and even on the ground. Not a great idea, I thought, remembering Lekule's story about the lioness.

Clouds, moving in since morning, now turned to rain, which continued intermittently through the night. It was cold, the temperature dropping to forty degrees Fahrenheit. At this altitude, many people—particularly those who have over-exerted themselves—begin to experience their first headaches and nausea. I was still OK.

The next day we would climb to Kibo Hut, at 15,500 feet. It would take five or six hours to cover eight difficult miles. This was the trek that nearly did me in a year ago.

I remember starting off somewhat energetically and, a few hours later, reaching a hill where Kilimanjaro's peak came majestically into full view. As we came down the hill, the landscape revealed a lifeless desert that grew visibly steeper as we slowly climbed upward toward Kibo Hut.

Mount Kilimanjaro is actually made up of two peaks. Mount Mawenzi, a harsh, jagged pinnacle of 16,896 feet, is on one side, and Mount Kilimanjaro, the glacier-covered peak that most people climb, is on the other. The trail running between the two peaks is called the saddle. Never will I forget the last two miles on that first climb. My body was completely dehydrated because I hadn't drunk enough water. My head ached, I was nauseous, and my throat was so parched I couldn't swallow food. Never had I felt as physically drained as when I staggered into Kibo Hut, collapsing on a nearby bunk.

These thoughts were with me as I set out for Kibo for the second time. I concentrated on a slow but steady pace, drank all the water I could, and ate as many carbs, such as nuts, fruit, and raisins, as my body would tolerate. One small advantage: I knew what to expect.

As before, the first half of the climb was demanding, but doable, and I was feeling OK. We ate lunch on the hill I remembered from a year earlier, overlooking the desert with both peaks in view. This time, however, I forced myself to eat all the food I was offered because I knew I'd need the energy over the next few hours. After a twenty-minute rest, I moved down the hill to cross the desert leading to the saddle.

Desert temperatures at this altitude can vary greatly. On sunny days at any time of year, they can easily reach over a hundred degrees Fahrenheit and still drop below freezing the same night. But today I was cold, feeling chilling winds from the Kibo snowfields. Stones and boulders that had spewed out of the once-active volcano thousands of years ago were strewn across the desert. All was quiet. No birds sang. No insects buzzed. The only things that moved were the wind, clouds, and sun.

When I finally saw Kibo Hut this second time, I was encouraged. I felt stronger than before but had no illusions about how close the hut was. I knew it was farther away than it appeared. Last year, after seeing it, I thought it would take an hour. An hour later, it was still an hour away.

Now, although bone tired, I had some energy. It took me almost seven hours to finally reach the hut. But this time I didn't collapse. Good sign.

An hour later, looking back on the trail, I could see Dr. Gaxtie in the distance, trudging toward the hut. Remarkably, he had made it this far. He still looked determined. However, he would tell me that Kibo was the end of his journey. Looking up the steep trail to the summit, he knew he couldn't make the climb. "I feel good, though," he said. "I didn't think I'd make it this far."

At 15,500 feet—three miles into the sky—Kibo Hut has no electricity or running water, and the facilities are spartan. Each room has eight double bunks. I was thankful to have a bunk, since every one was taken.

Guides served dinner at five o'clock. No one ate much at this altitude. I forced down soup and tea and tried unsuccessfully to swallow some dehydrated pasta. I had no appetite. We spent the early evening putting on extra clothing and preparing our gear. The mood was quiet. People talked little as they thought about the climb to come.

The sun set quickly, and, within hours, the temperature dropped thirty degrees. I was in my sleeping bag by seven o'clock to be ready for our wake-up call at midnight. An hour later, we would begin our final ascent in darkness. For me, sleep was impossible. My mind raced, thinking about last year and my lack of success.

I must have dozed for a few hours because voices and shuffling feet awoke me. A figure entered the room with a lantern swinging eerily. It was Lekule.

"Time to go, Papa. Get dressed, I bring you food," he said.

Obediently, I unzipped my sleeping bag and was soon sitting on the edge of the bunk adjusting to the dancing shadows cast by the lantern. Except for my boots and cold weather gear, I was already dressed. Most climbers sleep in their clothes to ward off the cold and be ready for the climb.

I ate a few biscuits and drank some tea. That was all I could handle. Wordlessly, I followed Lekule, his lantern swinging in the darkness. We joined Millard and started up the mountain. It was 1:30 AM and twenty-eight degrees Fahrenheit.

Again, my thoughts turned to this time last year. *I had been sick with nausea and a headache, but mostly exhaustion. Collapsing in the bunk that afternoon, I decided not to climb farther. Lekule had urged me to eat something and see how I felt by midnight. Reluctantly, I agreed and ate some stew. By midnight, I hadn't felt much better, but the thought of coming halfway around the world to climb a mountain and then not even try bothered me. So I'll try, I thought. I got dressed in slow motion, thinking that if I could just get on the trail, at least then I would have made an attempt.*

But, surprisingly, as I got out into the cold air, the nausea and headache began to disappear and I found myself with energy. Not much, but some. I seemed to have gotten a second wind and, after an hour on the trail, cockily thought I might even make it to the top. But that was not to be.

Here I was a year later, going up that familiar route, walking hypnotically behind Lekule, who was holding the lantern in the cold darkness. I was drinking water often and eating carbs. I could almost feel the new energy from the food kick in for brief spurts. The pace was slow but steady. Polé, Polé. Not to win the race, but to endure.

The stars were brilliant and large against an ink-black sky. The lights of the little village of Moshi twinkled sixteen thousand feet below us. I wanted to gaze further, but that would be a distraction, I thought. Concentrate on your steps. Measure them. Left. Right. Left. Right. Conserve energy. Follow Lekule.

It was getting colder. The wind was also stronger. Suddenly, Lekule's lantern blew out, and we were in total darkness. Luckily, however, I had a miner's light on my head, which I now splayed on the trail in front of Lekule.

Minutes later, we heard voices of people who were coming down the trail. I looked up to see a guide holding the arm of a young woman in her thirties. Her mouth was agape. She was hollow-eyed and seemed dazed as they descended. Probably from altitude, I thought. I would see eight more people descending before that night was over.

The air was very thin now, and the trail much steeper. I was breathing rapidly and filling my lungs with as much oxygen as I could. Even so, my breathing was labored.

I was tired. We rested for ten minutes on some rocks. We couldn't stay long because weather that cold can sap one's energy quickly. Just below seventeen thousand feet, Lekule informed me that this was as high as I had gotten last year.

My memory of that night, a year ago, was still clear: *I had lost my second wind and was tiring quickly. I saw a cabin. It looked like a warm cabin. Then I saw Lekule go in, and I wanted to go in too to get warm. But there was no cabin. "Papa, I'm right here. There's no cabin," Lekule said. He was sitting right next to me. I was hallucinating. I knew then I was in trouble, as did he, and further heroics to reach the top could be dangerous.*

But that was then. This was now.

We reached seventeen thousand feet, halfway to the summit from Kibo. At over three miles high, we were close to where jets flew on their way to Nairobi. Hans Meyer Cave, a landmark, is a simple undercut in the rock that serves as a final rest stop for climbers on their way to the top. It was named for Hans Meyer, a German geologist, who, in 1899, became the first person to climb Kilimanjaro.

As we sat in the cave, we could see early signs of dawn moving across the horizon. Darkness was giving way to a magnificent red glow that flooded the valley thousands of feet below. It was spectacular. We got our first glimpse of the sun as we dragged ourselves out of the cave for the final push.

We were now climbing on scree, a river of small, loose stones that can make climbing difficult. With every two steps, I'd slide back one. It consumed valuable energy, yet there was little I could do except climb more slowly. I now realized the benefits of climbing at night, when the scree was frozen.

I looked upward to the summit and saw doll-sized figures in colorful parkas moving in what appeared to be slow motion near the top. Now I was getting excited. *My God, there it is!* I thought. *There's Gilman's Point, the rim of Kilimanjaro. All I need to do is to keep moving and I'll make it!* However, once again, perception was not reality. After an hour of climbing, it seemed I'd gone no farther than a hundred feet. To make it to the top, we had to switch back and forth across the face of the mountain because of the steep incline and the ubiquitous scree.

The sun was hotter now, forcing me to shed layers of clothing. I was also having trouble breathing. Close to eighteen thousand feet, I had to consciously stop after each step. Movement was incredibly slow. My food was gone, and I was down to half a canteen of water. I noticed that several small figures above me had reached the top. Looking around, I found myself conspicuously alone on the scree, virtually inching my way up.

The final obstacle to the summit, which had not seemed so formidable from below, was a gauntlet of large boulders surrounding the crater's rim. It seemed almost as if some demented giant had placed them there to frustrate final access to the top. With oxygen levels at forty percent of what they are at sea level, I began to hyperventilate and had to rest even more frequently. It had taken me two and a half hours to climb 1,600 feet—a distance I had thought I'd cover in an hour. It was also getting late, and clouds were starting to move in around the mountain, a signal for climbers to descend.

But at this stage, I was thinking, *No way will I stop. I can see it! Maybe a hundred feet away. One step at a time. Breathe. Concentrate. Grab where you must—but don't screw up. And, for God's sake, don't fall backward. You'll never get up.*

And so the mind games went. Then, suddenly, I looked up, and I was there—on the crater's edge. Lekule, who had climbed ahead, magically appeared, waiting for me with his hand extended in congratulations. Smiling, he said, "Karibu, Papa, karibu! You now a son of Tanzania,"

Gasping, I mumbled thanks before collapsing on the rocky top of Gilman's Point.

Twenty minutes later, my breathing improved enough to get up and look around. The view was stunning. A field of glacial snow and ice covered the center of the crater. The white ice stood in sharp contrast to the colorless scree field I had just climbed below. Inside the crater were five-or six-foot-thick walls of blue ice. Condensation vapors from the glacial ice were majestically floating up and over the two-mile-wide crater.

It was 10:30 AM. I'd been climbing for ten hours, probably three or four hours longer than most climbers. I was the last to reach the top, but I was there. Physically, it was the hardest thing I had ever done in my life, and yet the most exhilarating.

For the next thirty minutes, I was content to sit and stare at the glacial panorama around me. I smiled at nothing in particular. I guess the occasion called for it.

Lekule came over.

"Time to go down. Clouds moving in," he said. Then he paused and looked at me curiously. "You OK, Papa?" he asked.

"Yes, Lekule," I replied. "Never better.

Let's go down!"

Above the clouds

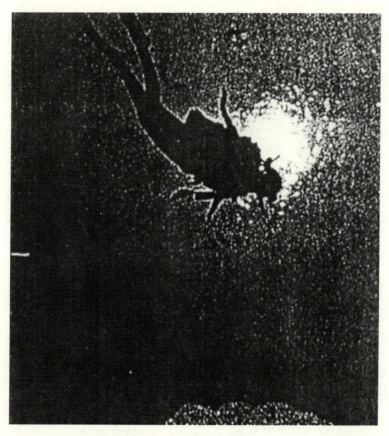

Diving

SCUBA CERTIFICATION

Some years back, I found myself on the small island of Bimini, north of the Grand Banks in the Atlantic Ocean. I was a day early for a three-day business meeting. I thought I'd explore the island.

While walking along a pristine, spotless beach, my eye caught a crude sign across the road: "SCUBA DIVING." Since I had always wondered what it would be like to scuba dive, I walked over to the small dive shop. Soon I was talking to Karl, a tall, twenty-year-old student who was working at the shop to defray his college expenses.

I liked what Karl told me about diving, and soon Karl and I were in a small outboard motorboat, heading for a dive location in the Atlantic Ocean.

"OK, Mr. Mac Isaac," Karl said when we reached our target, "I think you're set to go. Sit on the side of the boat and just roll backwards into the water when I tell you to. After that, I'll track you from the boat."

I did as instructed and, within minutes, had descended to about twenty-five feet. After the first shock of hitting the water, I was completely disoriented. It was a new experience, and, at first, I was apprehensive. However, during the descent I found myself surrounded by schools of brightly-colored fish. They were darting all around me like a welcoming committee.

As Karl had explained, my first order of business underwater was to make sure that my breathing equipment was working properly. It was, and I could also see the reassuring outline of Karl watching me from above.

The longer I was underwater, the more relaxed I felt. Adding to the experience were the sun's rays, which penetrated the water to reflect a stunning pallet of colors. After twenty minutes of exploration, I decided to find a memento of the dive that I could bring back to Judy. I looked around and spotted a colorful conch shell on a nearby reef. I swam to the shell and examined it. I must have been preoccupied because all of a sudden I discovered that I wasn't alone.

Sensing a presence, I turned around to see a very large fish swimming slowly, directly behind me—no more than five feet away. The fish was uncomfortably close and not in the least spooked by my presence, as were most of the other fish around me.

At first I wasn't sure what it was. It looked like a giant eel, but its mid-section was too large. Then I saw a mouthful of the sharp teeth and realized it could be a barracuda. The fish appeared to be about four feet long, and, eerily, it was maintaining my rate of speed. If I stopped, it stopped. I was scared.

I would learn later that there are seven species of barracuda that swim American waters. The Great Barracuda, the largest of these fish, can grow to over five and a half feet. Often called "tiger of the sea," the fish is predatory, fearless, and destructive. The barracuda usually feeds on other fish but will attack man. It has strong jaws and razor-sharp teeth that can be as long as three-quarters of an inch.

Had I known the Great Barracuda existed at the time, I probably would have panicked. As it was, I listened to my instincts and got out of there. As I swam slowly to the surface, the fish must have lost interest—thank God—because it suddenly dropped down and away, disappearing as quickly as it had come. My relief was palpable. I will never know whether it was a Great Barracuda, but it was one very large fish. During that brief encounter, I realized how vulnerable I was underwater. I vowed to never again go diving without professional instruction.

Little did I know how that vow would play out years later.

Coming home from work at IBM one night, I saw my fifteen-year-old son Cameron sitting on the front steps waiting for me.

"Hey, Dad, Tom Russo and I want to take a scuba certification course at the YMCA. It's every Thursday night for ten weeks."

"Sounds good," I said. "How will you get there?"

Hesitating a moment, he said, "Yeah. Well, that's what I wanted to talk to you about."

Another pause, and out it came: "Could you give us a ride?"

"For ten weeks?" I asked. "And what do I do while you and Tommy are in the pool?"

"Yeah, well, we thought maybe you'd like to take the course too."

Getting certified for scuba was on my list, but I hadn't planned on doing it so soon. And I worried that doing it with my son might be awkward. *What if he and Tommy pass the course and I don't?* I thought. *Ugh!*

But then a more paternal instinct kicked in, and I said, "OK, Cameron. I guess we can do that. When's the first lesson?"

There were seventeen of us that first night in a small auditorium in the Stamford, Connecticut, YMCA. The minimum age to take the course was sixteen. Most attendees were in their teens. I was one of four seniors. Each weekly class, we were told, would take three hours, plus a final two hours for a check-dive in a nearby lake, for a total of thirty-two hours.

Our instructor, Frank Johnson, was a veteran diver who had taught the course many times. Muscular, energetic, and solidly built, he looked to be in his mid-thirties. At about five-feet-five, he had a shiny, bald head that reminded me of a medium-range missile.

The course was well-organized. Johnson integrated lectures and pool work to reinforce what he was teaching any given week. It was also apparent that he was a no-nonsense instructor.

"You'll do homework every week," he said, "and I expect it to be done. We'll test frequently on what you've learned, and these tests will contribute to your passing or failing the course. Not all of you will be certified. And that's as it should be. When you dive in deep water, you don't have the luxury of mistakes. Your life, or the life of a buddy, is at risk."

Johnson reminded us that scuba is an acronym for Self-Contained Underwater Breathing Apparatus. Scuba divers wear metal tanks that hold compressed air, and they breathe from their tank through a demand regulator, a hose that supplies the required amount of air.

We would be using open circuit equipment, the most common type of scuba gear. The diver breathes from a tank, and the exhaled air is released into the water. The first independent breathing devices for diving were invented in the late 1800s and early 1900s. However, the first safe and simple device was the aqualung, invented in 1943 by two Frenchmen: Jacques-Yves Cousteau, a naval officer, and Emile Gagnan, an engineer.

Johnson told us we'd be responsible for getting much of our own gear, such as the mask, snorkel, fins, and a weight-belt. We also needed a medical certificate stating that we were physically able to take the course.

In subsequent weeks, our group settled down to a somewhat predictable routine. Johnson would review the previous week's homework and what we would be doing in the pool that evening. And there would be many written tests.

Johnson also believed that his students should be prepared for any problem that could arise in a dive, especially dealing with equipment. At each session, he had us swim innumerable laps around the deep pool with equipment combinations, such as fins and snorkel but no mask; air tank, mask, and fins; or all of our equipment.

After each weekly class, Cameron, his friend, Tom Russo, and I would stop by McDonalds for hamburgers and Cokes on the way home. We would replay what happened in class—where we goofed, and where we did OK. It was fun and something to look forward to.

As with any endeavor, the more we learned, the more comfortable we became. Cameron and Tom were doing well, responding quickly and correctly to Johnson's questions. However, as the course got tougher, some students had problems. There was one drill where we had to pair off with another student and do several laps underwater with only a mask and snorkel. Divers were connected to each other by a nylon rope around their wrists. As usual, Cam and Tommy hooked up together, and I teamed with another senior. I'll call him Paul. What I didn't know at the time was that Paul was claustrophobic.

Everything was fine for the first ten minutes. I could see Paul clearly underwater through my mask, and he seemed OK. However, on our second lap, Paul became agitated. His swimming became erratic, and he was moving his head back and forth furtively, staring upward. He then looked at me—wide-eyed—and motioned with his thumb in the up position. He obviously wanted to surface, and we did so immediately.

We swam to the side of the pool, where Johnson, who had been watching the mini-drama play out, helped Paul out of the water. The following week we learned that Paul was one of four students who wouldn't be coming back.

As the weeks passed, the remaining thirteen of us became more confident. We had all done reasonably well on our written and pool tests. But we hadn't yet done "Ditch and Don" (or D&D), which is considered by many scuba veterans to be the toughest test in the course.

D&D required us to first swim underwater around the entire pool, wearing with all of our gear: oxygen tank, fins, mask, and weight belt. Then, without surfacing, we had to swim to the deep end of the pool, where we were to quickly take off all of our gear (ditch) and then, just as quickly, put all our gear back on (don). Only then could we surface. If a diver surfaced with any piece of equipment missing, he failed the test.

Standing at poolside, Johnson had a clear view of all of the activity at the deep end of the pool and was monitoring how each diver behaved under pressure. He knew from experience how quickly underwater traffic can become congested. In order to give each diver sufficient time for the test, Johnson had to start two divers at one time. This proved to be OK as long as everyone swam at about the same pace. But some divers took longer than others, and jam-ups began to occur.

I was standing on the pool deck with my gear on, watching the other divers, and waiting my turn. I felt a little like Dustin Hoffman's character in the movie, *The Graduate,* who stayed underwater in his wetsuit in his parents' pool to avoid talking to the adults at his parents' cocktail party. My thoughts were sharply interrupted by Johnson's voice.

"OK, Mac Isaac" he said. "You and Alan (another senior) are next. Into the water!"

I walked woodenly to the pool stairs with Alan. We entered the water and began our underwater lap. We had good eye contact with each other and set a comfortable pace circling the pool.

We completed our underwater lap in about eight minutes and were headed for the deep end to begin D&D. When we reached the deep end, I was surprised to see one of the earlier divers still there. He was having trouble getting his weight belt on, so now there were three of us in the same area.

Alan and I began ditching our gear, leaving the oxygen tanks for the last moment so we could maximize our air intake. I got my fins off easily enough but discovered that I had to practically stand on them because of their penchant for floating. I began to take off my weight belt—a simple task, normally. But this time it was a problem. For some reason, my balance was off, and I began to weave back and forth like an anemone in a storm.

Finally I got the belt off, but in so doing, I moved my foot, and to my embarrassment, saw one of my fins floating serenely to the surface. Since I had no time to reach it, I thought that my test was blown.

But then a strange thing happened.

I saw a hand in the water above me holding my fin. It was the diver who had preceded us. Obviously still in the pool, he had grabbed my fin on its flight to freedom and was returning it. *Bless him*, I thought. The handover was done in seconds, and to this day, I don't know if Johnson saw the exchange. In any event, he didn't say anything. And I didn't ask.

With hope for completing the test renewed, I completed ditching my gear, as did Alan. Then we began the hard part: donning. Once I got my air tank operating and could breathe again, my confidence returned, and I relaxed. At that moment, I knew I'd get the rest of my gear on and would pass the test.

Several weeks later, at Candlewood Lake in Danbury, Connecticut, Cameron, Tom, and I joined the rest of our scuba survivors for the final check-dive. Despite lousy visibility in the lake water that day (only half as good as the YMCA pool), our group encountered no major problems and, to everyone's relief, passed the check-dive and the course.

We would be certified.

FLYING a GLIDER

Plugging a pair of portable, twenty five-foot wings into the fuselage of a large glider was unsettling for two reasons: One, the procedure reminded me of my son's Lego set in the toy closet, and two, I'd soon be flying in what I was now putting together.

Assembling the Glider

Judy and I were at the Danbury, Connecticut, airport preparing for individual rides in a glider—or sailplane, as it's often called. It was a late summer day and our host (and ride-provider) was Dr. Bob Orth of Stamford, Connecticut. Bob was an orthopedic surgeon and friend, who periodically sparked my interest in gliding, or soaring, a sport in which he excelled. When he asked one day if Judy and I would like to go up in his glider, we quickly accepted.

A typical glider is essentially an aircraft that resembles an airplane, but, unlike Bob's glider, has no engine. Gliders fly on air currents as silently and gracefully as birds. Most gliders are towed by an airplane to about two thousand or three thousand feet before the glider pilot releases the tow. Level flight cannot be sustained without a motor, so the glider pilot must keep the nose of the aircraft pointed just below the horizon line so it glides downward. The force of gravity produces the speed necessary to keep the glider aloft.

Bob's glider, a Taifun 17E, had its own auxiliary engine that could be used for takeoff, or launch, as it's called. Once the glider is airborne, the motor could be turned on and off—an enormous convenience for a glider pilot. Just as the modern yachtsman has a motor to help with docking or maneuvering into port, some modern gliders have retractable engines to get them home if soaring conditions deteriorate.

Bob, who kept his glider at the airport and usually flew on weekends, was a veteran pilot who had flown combat aircraft in World War II.

Earlier that day, when Bob's disassembled glider was first rolled out of the airport hangar, I was surprised to see that the fuselage looked like an ordinary light aircraft but the wings were dramatically longer than any small aircraft I'd ever seen. Orth supervised the move. In his late fifties, Bob had rugged good looks and was about six feet tall. After I introduced Bob to Judy, my gaze settled on the multiple glider pieces that had to be put together. At that moment, I was thinking, *Maybe this ride was not such a wonderful idea.*

"Hey Don," Bob called. "Grab the end of that wing and line it up with the slots in the fuselage."

Silently, I did as ordered. As Bob held one end of the wing and gently pushed it, I guided the other end into its proper position. The wing engaged with an audible "thunk." Bob tightened the bolt connections, and we repeated the procedure on the other wing.

Slowly, our disassembled craft began to look like a real glider. Already I was feeling better.

After conducting a thorough visual inspection of the aircraft, Bob looked over at me and smiled. "Ready?"

"Of course!" I said, with a trace of bravado, and we both climbed into the cabin to get ready for our flight. The cabin's interior reminded me of a Cessna 180, or even a Piper Cub. But when I looked outside, there was no comparison. Our fifty-foot wing span looked enormous—probably twice the length of either of those aircraft. We also had dual controls, which allowed either of us to fly the aircraft. I liked that, since I was looking forward to trying my hand at piloting. Bob pressed the starter button, and the engine burst into life. We rolled down the runway. We lifted off smoothly and quickly gained altitude, leveling off at about 2,500 feet.

Looking below, I could see the airport clearly. Parked airplanes lined the perimeter, and a few planes were taxiing into position. Others were busily being readied for flight. It was an ideal day for our gliding adventure. My earlier apprehensions had all but vanished.

About ten minutes into the flight, Bob looked at me and spoke quietly: "OK, Don, let's live dangerously!" I nodded, and, with that, he turned the engine off.

Soaring high

Suddenly *everything* was quiet. I could hear Bob's breathing, as well as my own. We were gliding, I thought, *really gliding!*

There was no engine noise; indeed, hardly any noise at all. The only thing I could compare it to was a parachute jump I had made years earlier. My descent then was marked by the same eerie quiet.

Bob said that our immediate task was to find an updraft or a thermal—a column of warm, rising air. He headed for some rolling farmland typical of rural Connecticut. We could see hills and a few clouds in the distance.

"See those puffy clouds over there?" Bob asked, pointing. "That's often a sign of thermal activity. Let's check them out and look below those clouds for some lift to climb on."

He was right. Even before reaching the first cloud, I could feel the aircraft rising. It felt like driving a car fast over a small bridge with a high crest and experiencing a sense of weightlessness for a few seconds. Bob now banked the glider to stay in the thermal and gain more altitude. He wanted to get higher to see what other options he had. As we circled, the glider rose higher. For me this was a new experience—feeling an aircraft in synch with the warm, rising air outside.

Once in a thermal, a glider pilot will often circle tightly to stay with the lift until the glider is high enough for him to strike out in search of more thermals. Gliding flights can be simple local trips, as we were doing, or more ambitious efforts to achieve either high altitudes or long distances. The world record for glider altitude is close to fifty thousand feet, flown along the Andes mountain range in Argentina.

Bob looked over at me. He was grinning.

Puzzled, I asked, "What's up?"

"Want to fly it?" he asked.

A bit surprised, I said, "Yeah, sure." (*Actually, I wasn't sure, but I took cold comfort in the knowledge that we had dual controls, so if I messed up, Bob could always take over.*)

"We have good altitude now," Bob said, "so you can experiment a bit and get the feel of it. See that cloud to our right? Take us over there. Just move your wheel gently to the right."

I did so, and, sure enough, the glider responded smoothly by banking to the right.

Hey, this is OK, I thought.

"Glider 101" continued with Bob talking me through the various controls I'd be using. He told me how pressing one of the pedals moved the rudder, which in turn produced a yawing movement off to the side, so that we literally skidded through the air at an angle around the glider's normal axis. Turning the control wheel moved the ailerons the pilot controlled flap on the wings to control the rolling movements of the plane, causing a banking movement and turn. Moving the wheel forward produced a nose-down pitching motion and a speed increase.

Now we were flying directly toward the clouds that Bob had pointed out earlier. Reaching the first cloud, the glider once again responded to my touch and rose thirty feet.

"Wow! This is all right!" I said.

I felt like I was flying the glider and was in control.

"That was OK," Bob said, "but don't get carried away. Gliders can be seductive. Stay focused."

Looking down, I saw what looked like a major interstate highway. "Isn't that Route 84?" I asked. I often drove the highway to work.

"Sure is," Bob replied.

"Think we could find a thermal there?" I asked.

"Worth a try," Bob said.

Lining up on the highway, I eased the wheel forward to slightly increase my speed. My target was an invisible column of heated air coming up from a busy interstate highway.

I'm not sure what happened next, but I must have pulled the wheel back too quickly because we *stalled*. The glider began to dive. Worse, it started to roll. Landmarks below us that just moments earlier were so familiar were now spinning. *We are in trouble*, I thought. Thankfully, Bob took over the controls, arrested the spin, and stabilized the aircraft.

"Bob, I'm sorry. What happened?"

"You pulled the nose up too steeply," he said. "Remember, we maintain altitude by staying just a few degrees below the horizon line so gravity works for us, not against us. It's a common mistake. You were doing OK, and if you had had a few lessons under your belt, you would have known that the nose was too high."

He was quiet for a moment, then added, "Flying a glider is like riding up and down an invisible roller coaster, and, like a roller coaster, you learn quickly where the scary parts are and compensate accordingly."

Bob allowed me another ten minutes to fly some straight and level gliding, during which I stayed focused. After Bob took back the controls, he said, "Probably time to go back to the airport and give your wife a ride."

Our landing was no different than an airplane's. Once Bob checked with the control tower for clearance, he lined up his glider with the runway, restarted the engine in the air, and landed in the traditional way. Moreover, we weren't at the mercy of having to be towed, as many gliders would. We could taxi back to the hangar without coming to a stop on the runway and holding up other traffic.

Landing a glider without an engine would have been the same except that the glider pilot would have to glide toward a landing area at a steeper angle and then level off just before touching down. A number of gliders now have airbrakes, or what they call spoilers, that can be extended from the wings to make it easier to control the angle of glide during landing.

As for the errant pilot who flies too far from his glider port (or airport) and can't find enough lift to get back, he must choose a suitable field and land in it. This is not as dangerous as it may sound because gliders can land on just about any reasonably flat surface three hundred to four hundred yards long. Once on the ground, the glider can be dismantled, put on a trailer, and returned to the airport.

After we landed, it was Judy's turn.

When Bob turned off the engine, it was such a free feeling. Everything was so quiet. We were low enough to really see the beauty of the countryside. The part of Connecticut where we were gliding was undeveloped and just breathtaking, with the foliage starting to turn into its fall magnificence.

I told Bob we had friends who lived on Candlewood Lake and asked if we were near the lake. Bob said yes and took us there. The lake looked so blue and clear from the air, and I could see the houses dotted around it.

I took the controls for a few minutes when Bob offered. What a feeling I only wish we could have stayed in the air longer.

After our experience, I can understand why people get hooked on gliders. According to the Soaring Society of America—which has over 120 gliding clubs—20,000 glider pilots are licensed in the United States. The Federal Aviation Agency regulates both glider pilots and gliders. A person must be at least fourteen years old and in good health to be eligible for a glider certificate.

On the trail

DOG SLEDDING

"Why would anyone want to go dog sledding?" Judy and I are sometimes asked. In my case, I remember being impressed as a kid by movies where Clark Gable drove a team of huskies—led by Buck, the wonder dog—into the frigid night. Judy's interest was sparked by her love of dogs and stories about the Iditarod, that grueling 1,100-mile dog sled race across Alaska.

As a result, one cold January day, we found ourselves in chilly Ely, Minnesota (population: four thousand), about fifteen miles from the Canadian border.

Ely is also home to Wintergreen Lodge, known by many as the sled dog capital of the continental United States, and where we would be staying. Here, guests can drive their own dog sled teams under the watchful eyes of artic explorer Paul Schurke and his staff.

Schurke has led four dog sled expeditions to the North Pole and has trekked across arctic Canada, Alaska, Siberia, and northern China.

According to the lodge brochure, trips (ours was for five days and four nights) were designed for "people of average fitness, with no experience needed." I liked that. We were in fair shape for our ages: Judy was sixty-six, and I was seventy-one. We were not exactly baby boomers, but we were ambulatory. We learned later that the average guest age was about forty-two and ranged from eight to eighty. Sixty percent were women.

The Wintergreen mushing season runs from mid-January to late-March. We would be dog sledding in a pristine, untrammeled area known as the Boundary Waters Canoe Area Wilderness. Here, a million and a half acres of land and water have been set aside by the U.S. and Canadian governments to be environmentally protected for future generations.

We arrived at Timber Trail Lodge at 4:00 PM. Timber Trail was one of the smaller Wintergreen lodges. It was near Farm Lake, where "Dog Sledding 101" would start the next morning. We had a small cabin with two bedrooms and a combined family room/kitchen. The family room had a large, rustic fireplace, but we weren't there long enough to enjoy it. The temperature was ten degrees Fahrenheit—not cold by Minnesota standards, but a cold wave was expected that night.

Judy: Before our trip, we found that we could rent (or buy) the heavier clothing needed for such frigid weather at a large shop in Ely, owned and operated by Susan Schurke, Paul's wife. Susan designed and produced much of what she sold—particularly sweaters and outerwear.

We also learned that dog sledding was a family affair for the Schurkes. Bria, Paul and Susan's thirteen-year-old daughter had accompanied her father on several of his expeditions. We met Peter (seven) later in the week, dog sledding on the trail with another group like ours. He had his own pint-sized sled with a team of three dogs and was most impressive in handling them. After watching him for a few minutes, Don said, "I wonder what the five-year-old does in his spare time."

We met our guides, Karl Volmers and Peter West, both in their late twenties. Karl was soft-spoken and tall, with dark hair and a trim beard. He had recently graduated from college and was taking a few years off to enjoy himself before settling down. Peter was shorter, very energetic, and quick to smile. Both looked the part of savvy dog-sledding guides.

Later we joined our fellow mushers, a congenial group that included a husband and wife from Bowie, Maryland, and four businessmen—a father and son and two friends from Kankakee, Illinois. The men had been sledding at Wintergreen once before. They didn't seem bothered by the six hundred miles they had just driven.

A master chef prepared evening meals at the main lodge and delivered them to the other lodges for guides to warm and serve. Guides prepared breakfast and lunch. Over a delicious dinner of roast pork the first night, we got acquainted with our new companions.

After the meal, Karl talked about the dogs, what to expect the next day, and most importantly, how to stay warm. He also reviewed information we had been mailed earlier about the importance of wearing layers of clothing. A wicking layer of long underwear draws away the perspiration and keeps you dry. A layer of light and thick insulating tops and bottoms, such as fleece, keeps you warm. An outer layer of material, such as Gore-Tex, blocks the wind and sheds snow. We rented high-top, insulated boots with liners, heavy socks for warmth, and lighter-weight wicking socks. On our hands, we wore wicking liners under thick fleece mittens with a nylon shell.

When we left for our cabin that night, it was cold. It would later drop to negative thirty-one degrees Fahrenheit.

At breakfast the next morning, the guides encouraged us to eat as much food as possible, including fat. They explained that we would burn a lot of calories in the next week. Guilt absolved, we ate pancakes, sausages, bacon, buttered toast, jam, and cheese. We also filled our pockets with trail mix and energy bars to munch on the trail and to keep our up energy.

Now it was time to meet the dogs. Karl had warned us about the bedlam we could expect, adding wryly, "It doesn't last long."

Even as he spoke, we could hear howling from the kennels. Sled dogs bark when they're excited. They love to run and pull, and the anticipation of doing so is almost more than they can bear. And the excitement is contagious. It usually starts with one or two dogs and spreads quickly through the dogs and then to the people.

Wintergreen's sixty-two pure-bred Canadian Eskimo dogs range in size from fifty to one hundred pounds, and they can pull up to twice their weight. Bred for power, not speed, their pace varies from four to eight miles per hour, depending on snow conditions. This breed—the original sled dog of the arctic—is considered to be the "Sherman Tank" of the mushing world—not fancy, but steady, tough, and effective.

Harnessing the Dogs

We were all offered hands-on experience harnessing the dogs. We could do as much or as little as we wanted. We all wanted to be fully involved and got instruction and practice before taking charge of our teams. The names of our dogs were: Akii, Rock, Ellesmere, Baffin, and Narpa.

As the dogs barked and rolled in the snow, we were shown how each dog is individually harnessed and attached to a single gang-line, usually made of polypropylene rope. The gang-line runs the length of the team, extending from the back of the lead dog's harness to the sled itself. The rest of the dogs run alongside the gang-line and are doubly connected to it by a neck line attached to their collars and by the tug line that actually pulls the sled and runs from the back of their harnesses.

Our guides patiently helped us hook the dogs to our sleds. It was an awkward, unnatural effort. At times it seemed life-threatening. Trying to coax the front legs of a strong, barking, eighty-pound dog with sharp teeth and no patience into a small harness was daunting.

Fortunately, sled dogs like people, so they let us push and pull their legs into their harnesses without too much resistance. I was particularly impressed with Judy's zeal. She fearlessly dove into the fray with a harness-and love. She'd work patiently with a dog, talking to it like one of her grandchildren, until it was harnessed. Mentioning this to her later, she quickly replied, "The dogs were easier to harness now than on our first try."

Judy: At the main kennel, young pups ran loose until they were old enough to start training. Several pups would accompany us on shorter runs on the frozen lake, barking, wagging their tails, and rolling in the snow. They looked like round bundles of fur with white muzzles and big blue eyes.

The first two mornings we came down to the kennels from the Timber Trail Lodge, there were twenty dogs (five to a team for our four sleds). However, at the larger Wintergreen Lodge, there were sixty-two dogs in the huge main kennel. Each dog had its own house, although none stayed in it except during a storm. They preferred sitting on top of their houses, which gave them a better view of the world. It also made for quite a sight as we approached the kennels.

And what a din they made. From a distance, they sounded like wolves. Our guide, Peter, explained that the dogs love to see people because they associate them with a run, which they love. The dogs engage in a deafening "group howl" in anticipation of running.

Dogs are trained with special equipment during the summer season, and their diet is lighter at that time. During the "mushing," or winter, season their food is increased to a high-fat stew made of raw meat, high-protein dog food, and lard. This is mixed with the lard to help the dogs maintain their fatty insulation layer and provides energy. Sounds awful, but they love it.

Judy: Harnessing a sled dog reminded me of trying to dress Molly, our nine-month old granddaughter, when all she wanted to do was get down and play.

Dog harnesses are made of reinforced webbing and have to fit snugly to prevent chafing. They go around the dog's neck so that the weight of the sled is pulled by the dog's chest. The two front legs go into special openings in the harness. That's the tricky part.

Don and I got a little better each day, but I doubted we'd ever be hired as dog handlers.

When a sled was ready to leave the staging area for Farm Lake, about a hundred yards away, it would take off like a rocket amid a tumult of shouting, howling, and barking. Judy and I were on one of four sleds that were lined up, one behind the other, on the frozen lake. As soon as our guides took positions in front and back of us on cross-country skis, we were off. Karl, the lead guide, broke up the trail to help the dogs, particularly in deep snow. Peter, in the rear, would trouble-shoot for problems like dog fights and potential frostbite among us rookies. Both guides had walkie-talkies to keep each other informed.

It was a clear, crisp day with a cloudless blue sky over a snow-covered lake. And we were dog sledding for the first time ever. We were at peace with the world. The dogs grew surprisingly silent. It seemed that once we got underway, they quieted down in their happiness to be going somewhere.

In our team, Akii and Rock were the lead dogs. We soon realized that Akii was boss. Even though at fifty-five pounds she was the lightest of the dogs, she was clearly the smartest and the leader. She set the pace and unerringly followed the trail being made by Karl.

Next to her was Rock, a big male dog, over ninety pounds, who, happily for us, had a nice disposition. Ellesmere and Baffin, with thick, snow-white fur, were our wheel dogs—those closest to the sled and us. Wheel dogs are usually the strongest in the team because they have to pull more sled weight. Ours were also brothers, and, as such, fought often. Narpa, our swing dog—in the center of the team—was the most impatient. He was first to howl if the team stopped and would futilely hurl himself at his harness to try and get us going again.

After a while, our caravan fell into a rhythm on the hard-packed snow. The sleds were usually in view of one another, and Judy and I had grown comfortable with our team. Standing side by side on the footboard and holding our handlebar, either of us could use the brake by stepping back with our feet on a metal flap, under which were spikes that dug into the snow when pressure was applied.

Most of the time, we used the brake to slow the dogs and keep them from tiring themselves. Usually one foot on the brake was enough. For a complete stop, we would both step on the brake shouting, "Whoa!" to the dogs. To resume sledding, we'd shout "Ready!" then, "Hike!" and the dogs would be off.

Our destination that first day was Murphy Falls, a small waterfall about a mile into the woods. To get there, we had to traverse a small peninsula jutting into the frozen lake.

For the first time, our sleds were on a rocky land trail with moguls and low-hanging branches. We had to crouch, shift our weight, and be alert to every turn in the trail. Each of us fell off a few times where the trail narrowed, but no harm done.

Looking across the lake, we saw smoke rising invitingly from the campfire that the guides (who went ahead of us) had made along the lakeshore. After a lunch of hot soup and nutritious snacks—eaten standing up because of the cold—most of us took the two-mile hike to Murphy Falls. There we saw a natural winterscape of the frozen waterfall surrounded by snow and trees frozen by the sub-zero temperature.

Judy: On the hike back, we heard fierce howling from the dogs. The guides had parked the sleds on the shore of the lake and unhitched all the dogs from the sleds, but they kept them in their harnesses, tethered to the trees. That allowed the dogs to check out the area, engage in friendly play, or just rest. As we approached the campfire, we saw a strange sight. All twenty dogs were standing facing the same direction, ears back, noses pointed high, howling. Karl thought they smelled a deer or coyote. It was quite a scene.

Back on the lake, we cleaned up, packed our gear into the sleds, and headed for the lodge. It wasn't long before we noticed the sun going down, and it quickly got colder. We stayed comfortable by pulling on extra layers of clothing that we had packed.

As we got closer to the lodge, the dogs picked up the pace. They wanted to get home. We had covered fifteen miles that first day and were tired. Yet, we were pumped up by the run. It had been a good day.

Dinner that night was chicken parmesan. It tasted great after all that mushing. The mood was upbeat. Everyone talked, often at the same time, about the run. Later that night, temperatures plummeted to negative forty degrees Fahrenheit, the coldest weather Judy and I had ever experienced. I had two sets of long johns, and I wore them both to bed.

The next morning, Judy and I did a little better harnessing the dogs. We took turns, with one of us holding a dog while the other put on the harness. Narpa wanted to roll in the snow, so I had to hold him between my legs so Judy could harness him. Not veteran mushers yet, but improving.

Our run that morning on Farm Lake was smooth and uneventful. We were heading for Crockett Lake, halfway to Wintergreen Lodge—our target. Shortly after leaving the frozen lake for land, we had our first accident. I thought our team was traveling faster than it should on the rough, snow-covered trail. Judy and I were standing on the footboard when, suddenly, coming around a sharp curve, our sled tipped, and she fell off.

"I'm OK!" she yelled as I looked back to see where she was.

With less weight to pull, the dogs were now running faster, despite my standing on the brake with both feet. Then I saw a rock on the trail and shifted my weight to avoid it. No go. The sled tipped, and I was thrown off.

As I fell, I saw the loose drag-line that is always attached to the end of a sled, and I instinctively grabbed it. With the line in both hands, I was now being dragged like a trail-sweeper behind the sled. I think my intent was to provide enough resistance to slow the dogs and prevent a runaway sled. But I can't be sure. Everything was happening too fast. One thing was sure: This was going to be one clean trail!

Just as I decided to let the rope go, the dogs stopped. Dramatically. There was another sled in front of us that also had a problem, and they had stopped—effectively, unlike us—blocking the trail.

My ride was over, and, except for a few bumps, neither Judy nor I were hurt. The problem, we concluded, was that we didn't have enough room on the footboard to shift our weight when facing obstacles on a narrow trail.

After that, we decided that when we saw obstacles, one of us would take turns jumping off, allowing the other to handle the team. Then, once past the obstacle, the sled could be stopped—thus permitting the jumper to hop back on. That approach worked. We fell no more.

On our last day, we awoke to a delightful surprise. Looking out our second floor bedroom window over the lake, we were greeted by an almost perfect, Hollywood-like snowfall. There aren't many winter scenes prettier than a dog sled running in falling snow, so after breakfast we all headed for the lake to harness our teams for the last time.

As usual, the dogs were happy. They eagerly followed Karl as he broke trail. Now and then, a team would run off into the deep snow until the mushers shouted and pulled them back. Judy's guess: They just wanted to play in the snow like any other four-year-old. As we mushed our dogs in the softly falling snow, I felt transported in time. It was another era, and I was carrying badly needed serum to Nome, Alaska. Or was it food to gold miners trapped in a blizzard? No matter.

My dogs were strong, sturdy, and brave; the sled was an irresistible force; and I yelled—as Clark Gable might, "Hike, Akii! Hike, Ellesmere! Hike, Narpa!"

OLYMPIC GAMES
(Winter 1980)

Listing *See an Olympic Games* as a goal was easy, but I hadn't the slightest idea how we might accomplish it. In fact, it was unlikely, since the Olympic Games are mostly held outside the United States, and the overseas venues would probably be out of the question financially. But the notion was not to worry about problems at the goal-making stage; it was to get ideas on paper. The realities of reaching them would come soon enough.

Coincidentally, this idea about goal-setting was reinforced some months later when I happened to read an article in *Reader's Digest* about a woman setting goals. In addition to listing her goals, she wrote about her cousin, who had accomplished an amazing string of interesting things by mentally preparing for the goals, so that life could work in its own mysterious ways.

"If you want your ship to come in," the cousin said, "you must build a dock."

I liked that idea and thought that my list of goals was a step in the right direction.

In April of 1979, I was managing a program for IBM's annual Corporate Recognition Event at the Waldorf Astoria Hotel in New York City. The three-day event recognized IBM's top performing employees from around the world for their technical achievements in previous year. One of the highlights of the meeting would be a film, for which I was responsible.

I had been working on the film at the time with a producer from Fort Worth, Texas. The working title was *Gymnast,* and it would highlight the 1979 World Championship Gymnastics competition that would be held in Fort Worth.

Our producer was also working on another film about the 1980 Winter Olympics that were being held that February in Lake Placid, New York.

Our schedule was tight. After reviewing the first edit of *Gymnast*, I requested some revisions that the producer agreed to make. However, he said that most of the editing would have to be done in Lake Placid, where he had set up a rented facility for the Olympic film he was producing. He said that if I could meet him in Lake Placid, he could make the revisions there and still meet my schedule.

I agreed.

Driving home that night, I realized that I'd be in Lake Placid at the same time as the Winter Olympics. Wouldn't it be great, I thought, if I could take a couple of vacation days after our editing was done and see a few Olympic events?

Then I remembered the *Readers Digest* article about "building one's dock" and had to smile. Hard to believe, I thought, but maybe life *does* work in mysterious ways.

Weeks later, I drove from our home in Connecticut to Lake Placid. The games were already under way, and the world was watching the various events and personalities. There were 1,100 athletes from thirty-seven countries participating, but the athletes that most captured Americans' attention were Eric Heiden, the twenty-one year old American speed-skater who would win five individual gold medals, and the members of the U.S. hockey team, a bunch of college kids who beat the unbeatable Russians.

Arriving in Lake Placid, I checked into my closet-sized room. However, I wasn't complaining because there wasn't a room to be had in Lake Placid, and I was lucky to get it. The weather was very cold—between five and ten degrees Fahrenheit—and there was a lot of snow on the ground. People were everywhere in the small village of Lake Placid, which had a decidedly festive air. Wide-eyed spectators and athletes alike compared experiences at the various venues, many swapping pins representing their countries or specific events. I heard music and laughter almost non-stop from restaurants and bars lining the main streets of the village. It was like a scene from a Hollywood movie set.

The next morning, I found our producer and his crew in the house they had rented for their Olympic film. "I could have *bought* a house in Fort Worth for the rent I'm paying here," he moaned. But at an Olympic Games, the laws of supply and demand prevail.

We went into their temporary editing room, where they were working on our IBM film. One of the editors showed me the latest cut of our film. It was much improved but still needed some work. I stayed with the editor most of that day at the editing bench. We agreed that he could finish the edits that night, and I'd come by the next morning to see the final cut.

I had dinner that evening with our producer, who told me more about the Olympic film. It had little to do with the athletic events but rather was focused on the arts, such as a series of musical presentations, featuring violinist Isaac Stern and other well-known musicians. were to be given at certain times during the Olympics. It would be these presentations he'd be filming.

Before leaving for Lake Placid, I had phoned my IBM manager and asked him if, after we finished the final edit, it would be OK if I took a couple of personal days to see some Olympic events. He had no problem with that.

The next morning we completed our final edit. With my work finished, I went looking for events to which I could buy tickets. Because I was late, most of the popular events were sold out. The most sought-after tickets were for the U.S.-Russia hockey game, a battle for the gold medal. Tickets for that game were $340 each, and every seat was sold. I heard that one lady wanted to see the game so badly that she offered a man $1,200 for his two tickets.

He said no.

I finally got tickets for two events: the men's giant slalom and the seventy-meter (230-foot) ski jump. The United States had never beat Europeans in ski jumping before. *Wouldn't it be great*, I thought, *if the United States could win a medal this year?*

And while I couldn't get tickets to see speed skater Eric Heiden (completely sold out), I did see him practice for his ten-thousand-meter race on the ice rink in front of Lake Placid City Hall. What impressed all of us watching this powerful athlete were the enormous twenty-nine-inch thighs that provided the strength for him to skate faster than anyone in Olympic history. No one else, before or since, has ever won five individual gold medals in a single Olympic Games. Heiden swept the five-hundred-, one-thousand-, fifteen-hundred-, five-thousand-, and ten-thousand-meter speed-skating events.

Courtesy of the 1932 & 1980 Lake Placid Winter Olympic Museum

The men's seventy-meter ski jumping venue, to which I had tickets, was a twenty-minute bus ride from the Olympic Village. Arriving at the site, I joined the crush of people heading toward the 154-foot tower, launch site for the world's greatest ski jumpers. It was clear and cold at the start of competition, with a gusty wind blowing behind the jumpers. We were all standing (there were no seats) as close as we could get to the barrier separating us from the landing area.

It was a new experience for me to see the world's greatest ski jumpers leave the ramp and soar through the air to their landing.

Among the first eight jumpers, the longest jump was eighty-five meters (274 feet). The maximum safe jump on Lake Placid's seventy-meter hill is eighty-six meters (275 feet). Beyond that distance, the terrain flattens out, and landing can be dangerous.

The ninth skier to jump was an American—Jeff Davis of Steamboat Springs, Colorado. He was an easy-going westerner who had had a number of injuries during his training regimen and had not been jumping well in practice. Expectations for him were not great.

He would say after the competition that he could hear the Americans cheering for him, and that the crowd pumped him up. With the sun behind him, Davis launched himself smoothly, his body stretched out over his skis. He held his form, soaring past the seventy-meter mark and past the critical point, beyond which the hill begins to lose its slope. The crowd let out a roar as Davis finally set down, wind-milling his arms to keep from pitching forward and eventually raising his arms in triumphant salute. He was in first place.

Five minutes later, the scoreboard went blank. The judges had conferred and decided that because of the wind, skiers were coming off the tower too fast. For safety, they moved the start several feet down the run. The round would begin anew; Davis' jump of ninety-one meters (298 feet) would not count. Americans in the crowd, including me, were devastated.

Davis later managed eighty and eighty-four meters (262 and 272 feet) on his next two jumps, finishing seventeenth for the best U.S. placing. Anton Innauer of the Austrian team won the gold medal with jumps of eighty-eight and ninety meters (290 and 295 feet). It was a big disappointment for the U.S. team, having come so close to a ski jumping medal for the first time in Olympic competition.

By the end of the day, busses were hopelessly behind schedule because of crowds exiting various venues at about the same time. Rather than wait, I decided to walk the five or so miles back to the Olympic Village. Many other spectators did the same.

The next morning, I used my last Olympic ticket to see the men's giant slalom on Whiteface Mountain. The venue wasn't that far from my one-room hovel, so within an hour, I was hiking up the mountain with other spectators to find a good spot to see the competition. Phil Mahre of White Pass, Washington, was the only American given a chance to beat the favorite, the legendary Ingemar Stenmark of Sweden.

The course ran down dramatic and steep terrain, forming a fast and very technical run. There must have been a thousand spectators lining the run. The course that ran down a dramatic and steep terrain, forming a fast and very technical run. Even as I looked for a place to watch, world-class skiers were whizzing by me down the hill to the shouts of their countrymen and other supporters. To find a good vantage point, I climbed higher, where it was colder (about ten degrees Fahrenheit) and more precipitous. I had on long-johns, ski pants and jacket, a scarf, boots, and my son's warm stocking hat, with holes for my eyes, nose, and mouth. I finally found a niche on the hill where I could see the skiers fly by.

Mahre had a great first run, sending gate poles flying. He was in first place by a full 0.39 of a second—unheard of for an American slalom skier. Spectators, especially the Americans, were exultant. Stenmark was in fourth place, 0.58 of a second behind Mahre. But then Stenmark produced another of his patented second runs, finishing more than a full second faster than Mahre to eventually win the gold medal with a combined time of 1:44:26 to Mahre's 1:44:76.

But Mahre won the silver medal that day—the first American man in sixteen years to win an Olympic medal in the slalom. The gate poles may have contributed to his missing the gold medal. The course gates were set with the old-fashioned bamboo poles, not the newer plastic poles that don't break, but rather pop back when hit by a skier.

In his critical second run, Mahre maneuvered a bit roughly through the first five gates and then struck a pole that became caught between his knees. It stayed there while he twisted through another three or four gates. Later Mahre said, "I was pushing myself too hard from the top, but if I hadn't had the problem with the pole, I would have fought it out. With my knees together, I just couldn't get rid of it, and I lost my rhythm." Seeing downhill skiers of this caliber for the first time—and so close—I was awed at the speeds they reach.

For millions of people, of course, the single, lasting image of the 1980 Winter Olympics was the infectious joy displayed by the U.S. hockey team following its four-to-three win over the Soviet Union. It was bizarre and beautiful. This was particularly true in Lake Placid Village, where a spontaneous rally choked the streets outside the Olympic Ice Center, snarling bus traffic for the umpteenth time. *This* was America's team. The fresh-faced U.S. hockey team had captured the imagination of a country. I heard impromptu choruses of the *Star Spangled Banner* in restaurants around Lake Placid, and there were reports that the U.S. players sang "God Bless America" in their locker room immediately after the game.

"Someone started singing as a joke, I think," one of the players said to the crowd at the Ice Center. "But all of a sudden we were all singing. We got to the part after 'land that I love ...,' and nobody knew the words. So we kind of hummed our way to the end. It was great."

I was unable to get tickets to any of the hockey games, of course, but the emotion and feelings the victory aroused affected everyone in the village. I was happy and unbelievably proud of our team and our country.

As I write these words, with the benefit of hindsight, it allows me to appreciate the good fortune of being in Lake Placid for that historic event. When I listed *See an Olympic Games,* I had no idea when, where, or even if that goal might be reached. But I think something does happen when a goal is written down. In some strange way, one's brain becomes officially imprinted with the signal to be alert to opportunity.

The dock is built and ready for the ship.

The MATTERHORN

With its snow-capped peak rising like a needle in the sky, the 14,692-foot Matterhorn is the most recognizable mountain in Europe. Straddling Switzerland and Italy, the summit looms menacingly over the little village of Zermatt. Here, climbers from around the world gather annually in July thru mid-September to try and climb this towering challenge.

Knowing that people die on the Matterhorn every year, I had concerns from the outset about listing the mountain as a realistic goal. But my inner voice said, *At least give it a try.*

I had climbed mountains before for exercise and satisfaction, but I had never performed a technical climb on rocks and ice, requiring ropes, crampons, and carabiners. Knowing this climb would be difficult, I decided on a two-year plan: The first year (1989) I would learn how to rock climb, and the second year (1990) I would climb the Matterhorn. It also seemed prudent to train as close to the Matterhorn as possible, climbing some of the less daunting peaks in the Alps to become familiar with the mountains and acclimatize to the altitude.

Jack Wheeler, a friend and world-wide adventurer who had climbed the Matterhorn, suggested that I hire Alfons Franzen as my guide. Jack, who remarkably had made the ascent when he was fourteen years old, used Franzen on his climb and was very satisfied. I'd later learn that Franzen was a legend in Zermatt, having climbed the Matterhorn over 450 times.

In the fall of 1988, I phoned Franzen in Switzerland, told him of my plan, and asked if he'd be my guide in the coming year. He was wisely non-committal, warning me that the Matterhorn is dangerous and not for amateurs. I'd have to be in excellent physical shape to climb it, and he advised me to exercise aggressively before coming to Switzerland. He would decide only after seeing me climb some of the easier peaks.

At the time, Judy and I were living in Wyckoff, New Jersey, a small town near the Ramapo Mountains, a moderate mountain range but a good place to train. I also found another training site: a former IBM building where I had worked for three years. The four-story building was all but vacated by IBM as part of a company-wide cost reduction program. I asked the manager of the small security staff that was still there if I could climb their stairs three nights a week and explained my goal. He checked with his managers, and they agreed to a limited time. For me, it was fortuitous finding a building with about sixty stairs to climb.

I also walked three miles daily and cycled six or seven miles four times a week. Judy and I worked out at a local gym using their Nautilus, treadmill, Step-Master, and weights. We also swam laps. On weekends, we climbed in the Ramapos, several

miles from our home. We would have a good hike and then a picnic lunch at the top.

As a warm-up for Switzerland, we decided to climb Mount
Washington in New Hampshire. At 6,288 feet, it's the tallest
mountain in the northeastern United States. It's sometimes called
the toughest little mountain in the United States, but not because
it's all that difficult. It isn't. The unpredictable weather, which can
change hourly, and the strong wind make Mount Washington
challenging. In 1934, the Mount Washington observatory
recorded the highest wind velocity ever observed by man—231
miles per hour, a record that still stands.

On our first attempt in late spring, Judy and I were halfway up
the mountain when a rainstorm hit. Soon the trail was mud, and
we were losing our footing. It turned cold—a raw, wet, windy cold
that penetrated our bones. After two hours, we decided we
needed to use a little common sense before we both caught
pneumonia. We went back down. Later that summer, we tried
again. The second time, I made it to the top and Judy came
close, reaching the ranger's station only a few hundred feet below
the peak.

September 1989

It was a rainy Thursday night when we flew out of JFK Airport on
Swiss Air bound for Geneva, Switzerland, and a new adventure.
We stayed in Geneva two days for some sightseeing, then took a
boat across Lake Geneva to Montreaux, where we overnighted.
The next morning we took a train to Zermatt and our destination,
the Perrin Hotel, where we would stay for a week to do some
climbing.

Tired from the day of travel, we crashed on the double bed,
hardly noticing our surroundings. At that moment, all we wanted
was sleep.

The next morning when we opened the drapes, we could not
believe what we saw. There, in its all its glory—perfectly framed

by our picture window—was the Matterhorn. For a few moments, all we could do was stare at this intimidating mountain piercing the morning sky. *How could anyone ever climb such a peak?* I thought.

After breakfast, I phoned Alfons to confirm our arrival. He sounded pleased and said he'd come by our hotel the next morning at 7:00 AM to pick me up. Judy and I now had the day to investigate Zermatt and our surroundings.

At 5,300 feet, the small a small Alpine village of Zermatt is free of automobiles and surrounded by more than thirty peaks over four thousand meters high (14,687 feet.).

Dominating the village is the Matterhorn, the Sphinx of the Alps, as it's sometimes called. The mountain is a magnet to mountaineers from around the world. When Judy and I took our first walk in Zermatt, we couldn't help but stare upward in disbelief at the over-arching presence of the mountain. While we found it strikingly beautiful, it was also a bit threatening.

We lunched at a small café where we could sit outside and watch the people walk by. Later, we did some shopping before going back to our room to relax before dinner.

The next morning, promptly at seven o'clock, Alfons Franzen strode into Perrin's lobby. He spotted Judy and me and came right over.

"Don Mac Isaac?" He inquired in a strong voice. (I almost wanted to say, "Here!" but didn't.)

"Yes," I said. "Alfons?"

I introduced him to Judy, who was interested in meeting the legendary guide. Franzen was a compact man, wiry and about five feet ten inches, with a craggy face, bronzed by the sun. His handshake conveyed strength beyond his size or age (he was sixty-five). My impression (which would later prove correct) was that few men of any age could match him on a mountain.

Getting right to business, Alfons said, "Today we will climb the Rifflehorn, a 9,600-foot peak. It will be a good climb for you." After a few pleasantries between Alfons and Judy, we were out the door and on our way.

For the climb, we took the Gornergrat, a cog railway from Zermatt to a location seven hundred feet below the Rifflehorn's summit, where we would start our climb. Surrounded by magnificent glaciers on three sides, the Rifflehorn sits just below Switzerland's highest peaks, Monte Rosa (15,199 feet) and the Matterhorn (14,687 feet).

The weather wasn't the best. It was raining when we left, but, as we reached higher altitudes, the rain turned to snow. Before climbing, Alfons had pulled a harness from his rucksack for me to put on. He carefully tied his rope to it, linking us together for the climb. He told me to follow him and do exactly what he did.

"Take small steps to maintain a steady pace and conserve energy," he said. I nodded agreement, and we started our climb.

At first it wasn't difficult. There was a trail of sorts winding its way up the mountain. However, as we went higher, the trail disappeared, and soon we were mostly scaling large rocks. I tried not to look down, preferring to focus on the steps Alfons was taking ahead of me. He moved with the grace and knowledge that comes from forty plus years of climbing. He also talked non-stop—directing me where to walk, how to move, and why. He was a good teacher. As I'd wait behind at one level, Alfons would quickly find a small ledge and the handholds needed to climb higher. He would take a safe, anchored stance and pass coils of rope around himself or a rock to hold (belay) me until I reached that position. Then, up again he'd go, while I'd wait.

Halfway to the peak, we came to a large, imposing rock—about sixteen feet high—that seemingly blocked our way. I didn't worry about it, thinking that Alfons would surely know a way around this intimidating obstacle. So I was surprised when he said, "Okay OK, Don, we're going to climb over this rock face. It's a bit difficult, but you can do it."

Oh! Oh! I thought, and my adrenaline began to flow. "A rock wall like this is not hard," he said. "You just have to find places for your hands and feet." Irrefutable logic, I thought, but I couldn't see any places for my hands and feet. I tried to look unconcerned, but I *was* concerned. Alfons was already on the rock, looking for microscopic cracks in its surface. His fingers were like tentacles clinging to the smallest crevice or protrusion. Within seconds, he was spread-eagled five feet above me—still climbing and talking.

"See, Don, it's easy. Just put the tip of your boot on this little sliver here. You see it?" I did. "Then put your other boot in this crack and push up. Understand? Use your hands only for balance. Use your legs to climb."

Mutely, I watched him scamper cat-like up the vertical rock face. I was sure his voice could be heard for miles as he told me everything he was doing and why. Suddenly, he was there. On the top.

As I looked up, sixteen feet above me, I could see him busily belaying our rope around a rock in readiness for my attempt.

"Now Don, y*ou* do it. And don't worry. I have you on the rope."

Wearing a fixed smile, I moved to the rock, looking for the places he used for his ascent. I found the first sliver—no more than a half-inch wide—and placed my boot tip in it. With directions from Alfons above, I found the tiny crevice for the other foot. Now, I was flat against the rock, hugging it, and turning my head anxiously back and forth, looking where to go next.

"No, Don! You're too close to the rock," Alfons called. "Stand up and out."

It was true. I was hugging the rock like a child clings to its mother. And, frankly, I was afraid to stand up—sure that if I did, my toes would slip from their delicate perch. After several false starts, Alfons directed me to the next set of toe holds.

I got the first one OK, but the other was two feet away, and I couldn't figure out how to shift my weight to it without falling. So, I hung there. I was only six feet from our ledge, but it seemed liked sixty feet. I was also losing energy. "Alfons, I don't think I can make it," I said quietly.

"Of course you can!" his voice boomed. "Just move your left foot a bit and you've got it."

I thought his confidence was misplaced, but it was easier to try, than to hear more verbal thunder. As I shifted weight, I lost my footing and fell. The rope held and Alfons lowered me to my starting point.

"Maybe I shouldn't have tried this one on our first climb, Don," Alfons said, almost apologetically, "but I wanted to see what you could do."

A mountain can be a tough teacher, I thought. You either make all the moves correctly or you don't. I didn't. And despite Alfons' conciliatory words, I had a sense of failure. Resuming our climb, I discovered, not surprisingly, that there *was* another way around the rock. He was testing me. We now moved toward the summit.

As we climbed higher, the view was stunning. The snow had stopped, the sun was out, and the leading edge of the nearby Breithorn Glacier was at our feet.

We could see miles of other glaciers, frozen rivers of ice inexorably inching their way down the Alps. Melting snow made some rocks slippery, so we had to be careful. Soon we could see the summit. When we finally reached it, I felt better about myself.

Alfons seemed friendlier as we sat on the peak for a quick lunch of trail mix, granola bars, and water. He had changed from teacher to companion, roles I suspected would change again. But, for now, it was time to savor the beauty around us. On one side of these spectacular mountains was Switzerland; on the other, Italy. However, despite the sun's warmth, we could see clouds moving in.

"We should go," Alfons said quietly. We put on our packs and headed down. We hadn't gone far when he stopped at the edge of the cliff.

"Now, Don, if you ever expect to rock climb, you must know how to rappel. And we're going to do that now." I knew that rappelling was lowering one's self with a rope down the side of a mountain. I had seen countless films of climbers doing it effortlessly. Now I wasn't so sure that it was easy.

I watched Alfons unwind the excess rope he had on his back, inserting a length of it around my waist through a belay plate, a friction device used to slow one's descent. The rope was also inserted into a permanent piton (a metal spike with an eye that's hammered into cracks in the rock). This arrangement allowed Alfons to control the amount of rope he would feed out as I descended. He then had me hold the rope and turn around so I was standing backward on the edge of the cliff.

Alfons said, "Now, Don, I want you to step off the cliff and walk down the rock face backward to that ledge fifty feet below. You see it?" I nodded and tried not to look down as I moved into position.

"Don't worry, Don. I have you belayed. You're secured."

I knew he was right, of course. Everything was safe, yet part of me (perhaps the saner part) didn't want to step off. But there comes a moment in one's life when you have to trust—when you have to step off. So, I did.

The rope held taut. *Hallelujah!* I thought. *I didn't fall.* I pushed my feet against the rock face and slowly began to descend toward the ledge below. After the initial fear, I began to feel better. *Hey, this is OK*, I thought. However, I was hardly a picture of grace when I came to large openings in the rock face and couldn't find a surface to push off on. I'd spin like a yo-yo, while listening to Alfons tell me what I was doing wrong.

"Lean back more, Don, way back, and you'll go down faster," he yelled.

But I didn't want to go faster, I thought. I just wanted to get there in one piece. Leaning back—nearly horizontal to the ground below—went against every survival instinct I had. But knowing it was useless to argue, I finally did lie back, and, sure enough, I descended more quickly. Reaching the ledge below, I felt great relief. I was silently congratulating myself when Alfons again yelled from his perch, "Not bad, Don, now let's do it again!"

I did. This time it was easier. No spinning. No slow descent. In fact, to the casual observer, it might have looked as if I knew what I was doing.

Climbing down a mountain, I found, was more difficult than I thought. Different muscles are needed and longer steps required. We were also facing out, so that I was now looking at the ground below and just how far down it was. We approached large, diagonal slabs of rock, all angled downward, and Alfons wanted me to walk down those rocks flat-footed.

'Don't worry, Don, you won't slip," Alfons yelled from above. "You have rubber soles! Just walk straight down!"

He demonstrated a sure-footed walk down the thirty-degree incline. I knew what he wanted me to do, having done it before on easier climbs in the Ramapo Mountains, but the consequences were lower then. If I had fallen there, it would have only been a few feet. Here, the stakes were considerably higher. Indeed, for me, the whole notion of walking down a slab of open rock, five hundred feet above the ground, gave new meaning to the word "fear." Overconfidence was never a problem.

Knowing that the matter was not negotiable, I started down. When I occasionally grabbed a rock to slow my descent, I'd hear from Alfons, "No, no, Don, don't hold the rock. Just walk down the rock! You can *walk* down!" With no small degree of acrophobia, I walked down, knowing that I was being belayed by Alfons directly behind me. After a while, I got the feel of vertical walking and actually liked it.

We were progressing nicely when, surprisingly, we came to the same large rock face that had defeated me earlier. Alfons stopped, turned to me, and quietly suggested, "Why don't we try this again?"

I didn't want to tell him I was more tired now than before and if I couldn't do it then, how could I do it now? I knew he'd think me a wimp, so I said nothing.

"Don, I think you can do it. You did well today. This was your only problem. Let's try it again." As usual, he was in no mood to negotiate as I watched him scamper up the sixteen-foot rock wall. Reaching the top, he looked down and said, "OK, you do it!"

I mounted the familiar steps slowly, reaching the point where I got stuck earlier.

This time Alfons spoke quietly, "Now, listen to me, Don. Push with your legs, so you're standing straight up. Then you can reach your next hand hold."

His softer approach must have helped because I found myself concentrating on his words. Slowly I began to stand, and, when I discovered that I wasn't going to fall, I thought, *My God, this is unbelievable. I'm actually standing on a half-inch ledge of rock.* It was like the feeling I got when I rode a two-wheel bicycle for the first time.

My confidence was building, but I still had a way to go. However, just knowing how to stand encouraged me to reach for the next two hand-holds and the next two steps, which got me higher than my initial effort. Although my energy was ebbing, I was now determined. Victory was too close to screw up. Alfons was supportive as I concentrated intently on the next toe hold to continue my ascent.

Suddenly I was there—at eye level with Alfons on his perch But I was also exhausted and could find no place for my last step—except the ledge where he stood. And that was too high. So, letting gravity take over, I slumped on the ledge.

"No, don't do that, Don!, You're supposed to climb to the ledge! Climb!" shouted Alfons, now back in character.

Clambering awkwardly up on the ledge, out of breath, I dimly recall saying, "Alfons, at this stage, I'll crawl to the top."

I thought I detected a slight smile on his face as I stood up and he congratulated me.

"See, I told you that you could do it. This mountain has every difficulty of the Matterhorn." He added quickly, "But, of course, the Matterhorn takes much longer and requires greater endurance." (As if to say, don't have any illusions about climbing the Matterhorn anytime soon, Buster.) "But you did OK."

Resuming our descent to the bottom, I felt good about the day. For most mountaineers, this would have been considered a modest effort, but for me, it was a big deal. I would later recall two valuable lessons: Experiencing and overcoming fear, and, surprisingly, finding that I could do more than I thought.

On our way back to Zermatt on the Gornergrat, Alfons said that my 'test' the next day would be to climb the 10,522 foot Rotohorn Hutte just outside Zermatt.

"You'll do this one alone!" Alfons said, looking straight at me, "I want you to reach the top within four hours. Phone me when you leave Perrin's at 7:00 AM and then phone again when you reach the top. There's a small restaurant, Edelweiss, on the top, and they have a phone. If you can reach the top in four hours, we'll climb the Breithorn (13,657 feet) the following day." That night, after dinner with Judy, I went to bed early knowing that the next day would be important.

The next morning I phoned Alfons at seven o'clock as instructed and told him I was just leaving. He wished me luck. The weather was good, and the mountain was easier than the Rifflehorn, but the climb was longer. The trail switched back and forth across the mountain's rocky face. There were other climbers, mostly locals, going up and down in an unhurried, casual manner. One could sense that this was familiar turf for them, and they paid scant interest to other climbers.

After an hour, I heard an extremely loud *whap, whap* sound. Looking up, I saw a giant helicopter with what looked like steel walls hanging under its fuselage. It appeared to be heading for a construction site up the mountain. (I learned later that it in fact was.) It was a surprise and a bit unsettling to see a helicopter fly directly over me, less than forty feet away. I would learn later that choppers are indispensable for any large construction in the Alps.

At 11:10, I called Alfons from the Edelweiss—ten minutes off my target of four hours. He didn't sound annoyed about the extra time. In fact, he sounded almost pleased, which, for him, was out of character. After we agreed to meet the next morning, I hung up and went looking in the restaurant for something to eat.

My choice of food was not the best. Thinking I needed carbo-hydrates for the hike back to Zermatt I ordered a large plate of pasta. I continued ingesting my energy drink that was high in nutrients, vitamins, and minerals. It was a decision I would later regret. For some reason, the energy drink and pasta was not a good combination.

Beginning my long descent down the mountain, I was recharged. I felt good about the climb so far and encouraged by my progress with Alfons. Already I was thinking about the next day and the Breithorn—one of the most picturesque peaks in the Alps. However, after an hour, my stomach began to cramp. And then I experienced the early symptoms of diarrhea. *Oh no. What a time for the trots! And I've got another two hours of climbing!*

Fortunately, there weren't too many people on the mountain, so I thought I could get down without too much embarrassment. I experienced the first nature call and had to quickly run to a large rock for cover. The calls that had started slowly now increased in frequency. Worse, there seemed to be more people on the trail. At times I felt like a mountain goat, jumping from rock to rock.

One close call came after getting off the trail and hiding behind a huge boulder from a couple who were coming down from the restaurant. The rock was between them and me and provided adequate cover. However, at the very moment when I thought I was covered, I heard another couple talking loudly in Ger-man—coming directly toward me from below. I had no idea how to hide from both. The dilemma forced me to move my body slowly around the rock in such a manner as to be hidden when the couples converged. One lady saw me, I'm sure, but out of pity or disbelief or both, said nothing. *Bless you, Fráulein, wherever you are.*

Hours later, I staggered into our hotel room and fell on the bed, briefing Judy as best I could on the day. After about an hour's rest, I began experiencing pain in my left kidney. Unfortunately, I have a history of kidney stones (about nine or ten), so I knew the symptoms. And this was a stone. On the move.

I immediately called Alfons and told him my problem and that I didn't think I could make our morning climb. In fact, at that moment I had no idea how this was going to play out. Based on past attacks, I could end up in a hospital. He was disappointed (no more than I), especially since things had been going so well and because losing one day would impact his schedule. Alfons and I reluctantly agreed to pick up next year (1990) where we left off. On that final note, we said goodbye.

That night I think I drank a gallon of water and was able to pass the stone by early morning. While I was relieved to pass the stone (and that the pain was gone), I was disappointed at having to cancel our climb. However knowing I'd try again the following year mollified my disappointment.

1990

August 1990 was the 125th anniversary of the first ascent of the Matterhorn in 1865 by Englishman Edward Whymper. That may have accounted for the increase in climbers that year. Sadly, within the first four weeks of that summer, the mountain claimed ten climbers. All had gone up without a guide, and eight of the climbers died on Hörnli Ridge, the normal route to the summit, and the route I was to take.

Zermatt guides pride themselves on not having had a fatal accident in forty years. They maintain their record by taking up

only fit and experienced climbers and—perhaps more importantly—knowing when to turn back. The mountain can turn into a
death trap—and does—claiming an average of one life a week
each summer.

From the valley floor in Zermatt, parts of the ridge look unscal-
able. They are extremely exposed, and, even in summer, the
upper sections are often coated in a treacherous layer of ice. At
any stage in the four-hour ascent, one slip can send an un-roped
climber over the edge, falling 3,300 feet onto the glaciers.

The climb up the Matterhorn starts from Hornli Hutte on the
lower spur of the ridge at 10,695 feet. It can be reached from Zermatt on foot. Usually climbers set off in the dark, at 4:00 AM.
They need to be well above the final refuge—Solvay Hut at
13,133 feet—by the time the sun hits the mountain. At that point,
they approach the hardest part of the mountain: the shoulder.
There, years ago, four of Whymper's party plunged to their
deaths down the north face. The Englishman's part in the accident remains controversial in Zermatt, even now. One version of
events says he cut the rope from which the climbers hung. This
section is now protected with a cable-thick rope, but it is meant
only to provide help and reassurance and not a means of pulling
oneself up.

Judy and I arrived in Zermatt in mid-August of 1990, staying
again at Perrin's Hotel. Because we were repeat lodgers, we got
an even nicer room than the year earlier. The couple who ran the
hotel was quite friendly, and, as before, we had a spectacular
view of the Matterhorn just outside our window.

I immediately phoned Alfons, only to find that he was booked
up for the next several days. However, he recommended another
guide, Charlie Schuf, who Alfons thought would work well with
me. I called Schuf and we agreed to meet the next day at Perrin's. Judy and I took a hike that afternoon and took it easy in the
evening.

The next morning—as with Alfons a year earlier—Charlie walked into Perrin's Hotel, promptly at 7:00 AM. He was much younger than Alfons but appeared to have the same energy level. About five-foot-ten, he was well-built and solid. As before, there was little small talk, and he and I were soon out the door heading for the Gornergrat. On the way, Charlie told me that we'd once again begin with the Rifflehorn, and if that went well, climb the Breithorn the next day.

The climb went extremely well that day, with Charlie and me climbing generally in the same areas as I had done with Alfons a year earlier. However, this time I found myself more relaxed and confident, which I credited to increased exercise during the past year. Having already climbed the Rifflehorn the year before certainly didn't hurt. From Charlie's comments, I could tell he also thought it was a good day.

At dinner in the hotel that night, Judy and I were surprised to see Charlie walk into the dining room with a knapsack in his hands and a big grin on his face. He wanted me to have it for our climb the next day. It was a brief but upbeat conversation, and I was feeling positive.

The next morning, I met Charlie at the base of the Gornegratt, the cog railway that would take us to the Breithorn. However, something was different. Charlie's mood had changed. He seemed agitated, almost brusque, when exhorting me to keep up with him on the crowded ramp leading to the Gornergratt. I didn't think the crowd was any larger than the day before, but he seemed to have a greater sense of urgency. I did the best I could to keep up but sensed it wasn't enough for Charlie, who was constantly shouting.

"Hurry, hurry, we must get a seat!" he said. There seemed to be plenty of seats, and we rode in relative silence to the level where we got off to begin our climb.

Climbers on the Breithorn

The Breithorn, at 13,657 feet (4,164 meters), is a beautiful mountain crowned with a magnificent mantle of glacial snow. From where we stood at the top of the cog, climbers looked like black dots on a white page. Because of the snow and ice, climbers must wear crampons, metal clamps that fit over one's boots and dig into the snow. For me, this was a new experience. At first I felt clumsy, but I eventually got used to them.

The Breithorn is less rocky than the Rifflehorn, but higher and, for me, probably more tiring. The continual effort of lifting each foot high enough for the crampons to clear the snow made the climb difficult.

Charlie was much quieter than the previous day, except when he was exhorting me to climb faster. He also seemed content to climb well ahead of me and then wait for me to catch up. The camaraderie of the previous day seemed to be gone. Several times, I felt that I was on my own, and, because of that, I made a couple of mistakes that burned up valuable energy.

I sensed that Charlie and I were no longer a team. I had the distinct impression that he was in a hurry to get this climb over with and get down. At one point, he told me he had some phone calls to make and hiked ahead to a small lodge on the mountain. Exhausted, I sat down outside the lodge to wait for him.

Later—riding the Gornergratt down to Zermatt—I wasn't surprised when Charlie told me he didn't think I was ready for the Matterhorn the next day. I was disappointed but too tired to argue. I don't think it would have made much difference. His mind was made up. It might have had something to do with the ten climbers who fell to their deaths the previous week and the legitimate desires of guides to take only their best and strongest climbers. I can understand that and respect it. The reality, of course, is that I'll never know.

After our railway car reached Zermatt, I paid Charlie for the climb and headed directly to the Mountain Guides Office, a short walk from the Gornergrat. Entering the office, I asked the head guide at the desk if a guide was available to take me up the Matterhorn the next day.

I detected a slight smile from the older man when he immediately replied, "Oh, no, no, too late for tomorrow! All guides busy. You're too late. You have to get your guide earlier. Much earlier!"

I was tempted to say, *I did that. A year ago.* But that would have served no purpose.

I thanked him and left the office to tell Judy that it was over. I would not be climbing the Matterhorn. It was disappointing, of course, because I honestly thought I had a chance to reach the top. However, I guess the guides knew best. Beyond my initial disappointment, I have no regrets. By climbing the Rifflehorn, I was able to accomplish something I had never expected to and, in the process, push my body to a new level of physical effort.

And that has to be worth something. Judy and I had an experience that we could only have dreamt about before.

And—I didn't die.

RUNNING the BÍO-BÍO

"OK, gang, battle stations," Mike Speaks said softly.

Judy and I, and Mary Cameron of California, were in wetsuits, seated in a fourteen-foot rubber raft. Mike, our Mountain Travel-Sobek guide, was untying the line that kept the raft safely out of the grasp of a swift current that raced into the fabled Lava South rapids.

We were on the Bío-Bío River in central Chilé, in the volcanic foothills of the Andes. The river is South America's most celebrated whitewater run, and for good reason. It contains some of the most turbulent rapids in the world. I first heard about the 238-mile long Bío-Bío (pronounced bee-o, bee-o) from Colorado River guides when Judy and I ran that legendary river in 1982.

We wanted to try it, but for a decade we dithered. One reason was cost. Airfare to Chilé at the time was about $2,000 for two, plus we would have to pay about $4,000 for land costs, which included accommodations, meals, transportation within Chilé, camping, and river equipment. The total trip cost would be about $6,000. It was much too expensive for us with three kids in college. So we decided to plan the trip after they had graduated. Yet, we couldn't wait too long or we might fossilize, unable to handle the physical demands of the trip.

So, a couple of years later when Judy was fifty-nine and I was sixty-four and our kids were out of college, we knew that if we were ever to run the Bío, now was the time.

Our fifteen-day trip in January began in the lobby of the Hotel Carrera in downtown Santiago, Chilé. There we met Stan Boor (pronounced Boar), our Mountain Travel-Sobek trip leader. When not running rivers around the world, Boor could be found in Alaska, building a house for himself.

We also met our eighteen traveling companions, an eclectic group that included a lawyer from North Carolina, a dentist from Zurich, a saleslady from Chicago, an exporter from Hong Kong, and a farmer from Colorado.

At the hotel, we were each given two waterproof black bags in which to pack our essential clothing and gear for the river. We would live out of these bags for the next ten days. Non-essentials were checked at the hotel for pick-up after the trip.

That evening, we boarded a sleeper train to Victoria, the closest railroad station to our target. We would get on the river at the Lonquimay (Lone-key-MY) put-in five hundred miles south of Santiago. The train, an old German diesel built in 1930, swayed and lurched noisily over its narrow-gauge track. Reaching the dining car was daunting, but our reward was a chance to talk to our new companions over steaks and good Chilean wine.

Early the next morning, we arrived at Victoria station and transferred our gear to a bus that took us to Manzanar, a little town at the foothills of the Cordillera mountain range of the Andes.

We checked into an old, rustic, two-story hotel surrounded by Araucaria pines, primitive conifers that are among the planet's oldest species. Some of the trees are one thousand years old. After a late breakfast, some of our group took a hike, but most of us retreated to our rooms to repack bags, rest, and enjoy the last hot shower we would have for weeks.

The next morning, we boarded our second bus in as many days for the three-hour drive to the river. Our destination, Lonquimay, was a small village just above Lakes Gualletue and Icalma ((Gah-yeh-TWEH and Ee-CAH-ma) at the headwaters of the Bío-Bío. There our rafts were waiting.

When we got to the river, even before our bus door opened, two of the five guides we would soon meet scrambled onto the bus roof to untie and throw down our black bags to waiting hands. Like us, they were eager to get on the river.

Between reclaiming our gear, trying on life jackets, and eating a tasty lunch, we eventually met our other guides. Mike Speaks, one of the guides, gave us a safety talk on such things as danger from the sun because of serious ozone depletion in South America. Speaks told us to keep our bodies covered, to drink only water that had been purified (with their portable purifier), to be sure to drink water often to stay hydrated, and to point our feet downstream and float to quiet water if our raft capsized.

Soon we were on the river in a flotilla of six rubber rafts. There were twenty-four of us—eighteen passengers and six guides. Judy and I joined Bert Mueller, a congenial ferry engineer from Gig Harbor, Washington. Bert was a large man, well over six feet and two hundred pounds. Because he had the only camcorder, he became the trip's official video scribe. His bright red hat would constantly flag his presence, no matter where he was on the river.

Our boatman, Butch Carber, was a seasoned river runner with whom Judy and I had gone down the Colorado River a decade earlier, so it was a chance for the three of us to catch up on the intervening years. He hadn't changed much. He was still lean, tall, and well-muscled, with a relaxed manner and a quick smile.

The day was hot, about ninety degrees Fahrenheit, but the constant slap of river water on our faces kept us cool. We three passengers sat in the bow of the raft to balance the weight of our supplies in the stern. Butch sat in the middle of the raft. The craft had a sturdy frame of aluminum tubing two-inches in diameter. The frame was lashed to the fourteen-foot, inflatable Zodiac raft.

The Bío-Bío's name is derived from the call of a bird, the Chilean Flycatcher. Already we were hearing the flycatcher's distinctive *bee-o, bee-o* call as we headed downriver.

Initially, the rapids were shallow as the river rippled through soft, rolling countryside. In the first twenty miles, we flowed past an alpine forest and a broad foothill plateau. Gentle banks and green fields gradually sloped to the base of the surrounding mountains.

Rounding a bend in the river, we saw Volcan Callaqui (CAL-a-key), a ten-thousand-foot smoking volcano. It was stunning and dominated the skyline of the Andes. We all gazed at the volcano without saying much until it disappeared from sight. Butch told us we would see it again, later in the trip.

Our first camp site was set up late in the day on a sandy spit of land. The guides handed out tents, and each of us looked for flat ground on which to set them up. The guides, all of whom were excellent cooks, prepared barbecued chicken, rice, and salad. Later, we sat around a fire drinking Chilean beer and wondering whether all the guides' dark talk about Lava South rapids was just hype to scare us. Consensus: It wasn't.

During the next few days, we splashed and careened through an endless cascade of rapids, some moderate and predictable, others deceptive and difficult. As we lost elevation, Araucaria trees gave way to cedar groves and cypress trees draped with Spanish moss.

We saw torrent ducks—thrush-like birds found only in Chilé—flying rapidly upstream, just inches above the water. We also saw swallows, finches, wrens, and black-faced ibis.

Further downstream, the river began to narrow. We noticed that the horses and sheep we had seen along the banks earlier had disappeared. Also, the river was becoming more turbulent. The rapids were coming.

Rapids are generally rated one through five, with six defined as unrunnable. Class five rapids, as defined by the American Whitewater Affiliation, are "extremely long, obstructed, or very violent.... Scouting is mandatory." We were now approaching Jugbuster, class five rapids at the halfway mark on the river. Over the years, various guides have assigned colorful names to the more difficult rapids, like including Milky Way, Lost Yak, Lava South, Joker, and Royal Flush. We were told that Jugbuster was unpredictable and dangerous. We would soon find out why.

Our rafts were tied up two hundred feet above the rapids so the guides could scout conditions—normal procedure for class four and five rapids. Since these were to be our first big rapids, a few of us—the more curious of the group—followed the guides to see for ourselves.

We climbed over large, slippery boulders that lined the river's edge. We reached a vantage point about twenty feet above the river, where we saw that new rock had fallen into the gorge. The rock squeezed the river channel to a dangerous level of turbulence. Water levels were so low that, in places, the rafts would have trouble clearing the rocks. After forty minutes, the guides decided that each raft should run as light as possible. There would be one guide and only one-passenger, the lightest and strongest from each raft. The rest would have to walk around the rapids.

Approaching Jugbuster

Judy and I were riding that day with Chris Grauert, a former carrier pilot from Fairfax, Virginia, and his wife. Chris had recently retired from active duty with the U.S. Air Force and was in great shape. Chris was tall, athletic, and the obvious choice from our boat to run the rapid. He would paddle with Jenny Gold, the only female guide on the trip.

We had met Jenny the first day on the river. Later, we learned that she was an experienced guide who, besides previous experience on the Bío-Bío, had run the Zambezi River in Africa. She was the first woman to ever row the turbulent Coruh River in Turkey. Young, strong, and hardworking, Jenny also led trekking trips in Patagonia and Southern Africa.

Judy and I were disappointed not to be running , but we knew it was the right call. Jenny told us not to be disappointed. The best was yet to come.

Everyone made it through without mishap, although there was an anxious moment when Mike Speaks' raft hung up on a rock for a few seconds. To those of us on shore, it seemed like minutes. A moment longer and Mike would have flipped.

Late in the afternoon, as we pulled into camp, it began to rain. And rain. And rain. We ran to get our tents up, but we were not quick enough to avoid getting drenched.

To keep our food and campfire dry, the guides set up a large tarpaulin, which also served as a dining room where meals were consumed standing up. Even though we were eating elbow to elbow and listening to the rain pelt our plastic roof, spirits didn't seem to sag. John French, a guide, kept us distracted with his marathon recitation of the poem, "Dangerous Dan McGrew." By the time he finished, the rain had slowed enough for most of us to retreat to our tents.

To break routine, the next day's schedule called for the option of taking one of several hikes, one of which was a strenuous one to the nearby Volcan Callaqui that we had seen earlier. The crater was at ten thousand feet. The hikers would reach base camp before dark and leave at 5:00 AM the next morning to make the final ascent to the top.

There were two other hikes: Climbing to the volcano's base camp or a half-day climb to a giant waterfall along the way. Since Judy and I wanted to conserve what energy we had for the river, we chose the waterfall.

The next morning was ideal for the hike with clear skies and temperatures of seventy-five degrees Fahrenheit. We all climbed the ridge that paralleled the river on our way to the waterfall, where we would have lunch. This would be the first stop for those heading for the volcano and the final stop for us.

Our trail tracked through dense forest and open countryside. With prior permission, we trekked through a large farm. Maria, its owner—whom the guides knew from earlier trips—was making *pan de horno*, country bread baked in an earthen oven. She waved hello and chatted with Stan and Mike. She was complaining about sandals she had received through the mail. The sandals were fine, she exclaimed loudly, but both were for the left foot.

Waterfall below Volcan Callaqui

The waterfall, like so many in Chile, was spectacular. It fell ninety feet to a gorge below, and really adventurous souls could crawl out to the precipitous lip of the falls and look down to the rocks below.

We had lunch and were joined later by some Pueneche Indians. Their horses would carry the gear for those heading to the volcano. The plan was for Butch Carber to guide Judy and me back to camp, where we would overnight while the hikers camped out at the base of Callaqui. The following morning, those who felt strong enough could try for the top of the volcano. Then all the hikers would return to camp.

I remember clearly the moment of the accident. Judy and I were heading down a moderate slope with Butch in the lead when it happened. Judy's foot slid on scree—small, loose stones that can be deceptively unstable—and she fell.

No big deal, I thought. Stumbles and falls are common to hikers. Except this one was different. Judy tried to get up and couldn't.

"Oh, oh," Judy said. "Something's wrong." I helped her to her feet, but she experienced a sharp pain as soon as she put weight on her foot. She took a few more steps and said with annoyance, "Damn, I think it's a sprain." What none of us knew at the time was that she fractured a bone in her ankle, something we wouldn't find out until we returned to the United States and had the ankle x-rayed.

The accident wouldn't have happened if Judy had had her hiking boots. But, since we hadn't planned to do much hiking, we had left our boots home to conserve valuable space in our black bags. We both had only sneakers, which didn't provide much support, for the hike.

Here we were in the middle of a Chilean jungle, about four miles from camp, no one in sight, and Judy could hardly walk. It was after 2:00 PM, and we knew we had to reach camp before dark. For awhile, Butch and I positioned Judy between us so she could lean on our shoulders and walk on her good leg. But when the trail narrowed, that didn't work, and she had to use her injured leg more than she wanted to. I found a large branch in the woods, which I fashioned into a crude crutch, and that helped some.

"I think I know a shortcut to camp," said Butch. "It might save us an hour." We thought that was a good idea and plunged into even denser forest with Judy now limping pretty much unaided. I became really concerned when our trail disappeared. Butch looked for places where it might resume, but no luck. Judy was sitting on a stump while the search went on.

"I think I've found the trail!" Butch yelled. Judy and I headed in the new direction.

"It's been a few years since I've hiked in these parts, and there's been a lot of growth since then," Butch explained. But even that trail played out. Worse, we found ourselves in some kind of a swamp with dead trees and bushes everywhere. Butch and I were now helping Judy over fallen trees and branches by passing her back and forth to one another. There was a moment when I felt like a U.S. Ranger in jungle training. I would have laughed were it not so serious.

Finally, Butch picked up the trail (thank God), and we made it back to camp. Judy was exhausted. To reduce the swelling in her ankle, Butch commandeered some frozen orange juice from the "dry ice" cooler on our raft. With his first aid training and a well-stocked emergency kit, Butch tended to Judy's ankle. He placed cans of frozen juice on the painful area and wrapped every-thing—towel, juice, and Judy's leg—with an ace bandage. We then elevated her leg on an "ammo" can (which kept cameras dry on the river), and she immediately fell asleep. Hours later, when she awoke, Butch brought her a steak dinner—complete with candles, taped music, and a bouquet of wild flowers.

The next morning, the pain had eased, and with the help of low-hanging branches and a crutch, Judy was able to make it from our tent to the river's edge to wash and brush her teeth.

After a breakfast of French toast, orange juice, and coffee, we talked about what would happen now. Did Judy want to cut the trip short and be taken out in a helicopter? If so, it would have to be tomorrow at the next put-in, a short distance down the river.

"No way, absolutely not," she said. "We've planned and saved for this trip for over a year, and I don't want it to end like that. I'll see Tom when he gets back tonight, and he can look at it." Tom Eckert, from Madison, Indiana, was a doctor in our group who was hiking back from the volcano. Judy added, "Tomorrow's a big day! Tomorrow we do Lost Yak and Lava, and I'm going."

She can be a tough lady when she needs to be.

The hikers returned to camp that evening. Except for the guides, who were all in good shape, our fellow companions were exhausted. Only five had made it to the top. All that anyone wanted to do upon returning to camp was eat and sleep. Chris Grauert, our top gun and one of the five who made it to the top of the volcano admitted, "That was the toughest thing I ever did in my life."

Dr. Tom made his tent call to look at Judy's leg. He thought it was a sprain, particularly since she was able to walk on it as much as she did. But without an x-ray, it was impossible to know if it was fractured. Judy promised she'd have x-rays taken when we got back to the United States.

It was settled. Judy was going to run Lost Yak and Lava South, perhaps the two most difficult whitewater runs of the trip.

Morning Mist

The morning was warm and hazy. As a few clouds floated lazily under a perfectly blue sky, we ate breakfast and packed our gear. Stan Boor reviewed safety procedures, this time in detail. He explained that, before each run, we would be told the conditions of the rapid by our boatman and where to swim in case we capsized.

"This is no Disneyland ride," Stan said somberly, "There's not always a happy ending on the Bio. Rafts can flip, as one did two weeks ago." He had our attention. "If that happens, keep your feet heading downstream until you float to calm water. As soon as you're there, swim for shore—unless you want to run down another set of rapids by yourself. We'll throw you a line. Grab it, and we'll pull you in."

"Finally," he warned, "secure your life jacket and helmet tightly. A loose jacket can slip right over your head if we're pulling you out of the water. That's what we grab, the life jacket!"

Sobering words, I thought. Yet, I don't think anyone was fearful. Concerned of course, but not afraid. After all, we were aware of the inherent risks of the trip. And, although always possible, serious injury was unlikely. We had selected an experienced company with a good reputation for safety. We were as fit as we could hope to be, and now we knew what to do in case of trouble.

For Lost Yak and Lava, Judy and I would be rafting with Mike Speaks, a well-built, bearded veteran in his mid-thirties. Speaks had run most of the world's great rivers. Actually, we were quite pleased to be riding with Mike. Months earlier, Judy and I read *Shooting the Boh*, an exciting book on whitewater rafting by Tracey Johnston. The book was a true adventure about Johnston's exploration of a virtually unrunnable river in Borneo. Johnston was lavish in her praise for the trip's lead guide—none other than Mike Speaks—who, she said, averted near disaster in several life-threatening situations. Johnston credited her survival to Speaks' boating and leadership skills.

A self-effacing person by nature, Mike found the spotlight's glare uncomfortable. He didn't want to talk about the book, and, while we wanted to ask a hundred questions, we deferred to his wish.

Mary Cameron, the third passenger in our raft, was a young film producer from California. She was attractive, outgoing, and athletic. She told us that she competed in 6K and 10K marathons.

Scouting is essential for Lost Yak, and the guides—followed by some of us, once again, scurried over silt-covered rocks for an assessment. That first view of rapids, as wild as I'd ever seen, was scary.

A 150-foot waterfall behind the rapids dropped from a sheer cliff to the river below. It looked like something out of a movie like *Heart of Darkness*.

Our guides took it all in and discussed their options. Some forty minutes later, they headed back to the rafts to brief us. We would go in two groups of three boats. This would permit guides from one group to provide safety backup for the other. Our raft, with Mike on the oars, would be the second through the rapids.

As we tightened life jackets and helmet straps, the mood was noticeably quiet. Most of us were in wet suits to maintain body heat in case we were dumped into the river. Judy's ankle was feeling better, she told me, but I wasn't sure I should believe her.

Judy: The most difficult day was when I injured my leg and had to do all that hiking to get back to camp. Once Butch ingeniously wrapped my leg with frozen juice cans, the swelling went down.

When we were in the raft, I could elevate my leg on the side of the raft, and the constant flow of icy cold water over the side kept the ace bandage saturated. "Ideal conditions," according to Dr. Tom.

It was disappointing to have to sit out some of the hikes, but we had brought a supply of paperback books with us. It was a nice respite to find a cozy corner in the shade along the river bank to curl up and read.

Lost Yak was named for a dramatic capsize shortly after the rapid was discovered in 1978. As the story goes, an unnamed kayaker was dumped into the froth, separated from his craft, and eventually rescued by other kayakers. He was OK, but his kayak was never found.

On our trip, Stan's raft went first. We watched it disappear as it fought the rapids, and reappear after the rapids, now farther away and smaller. When we later heard cheers down river, we knew they made it through.

Now it was our turn. Mike had me untie the bow line, and we moved quickly into position. The current was fast and immediately grabbed us. We were committed.

There were rocks everywhere. Mike pulled hard on his oar to miss a big one, but not soon enough. Thwunk! We bounced off its side, and the raft turned around just before dropping into a large hole. Instantly, we were inundated by walls of water breaking over us from all sides. It's unnerving to see a wall of water, six feet high, coming at you, ready to break. My knuckles were white from the safety line I held. Suddenly, we were spit out of the hole and, for a second, could see more boulders ahead—sentinels guarding a raging cauldron.

The river turned sharply, and there it was again: the 150-foot waterfall crashing from the cliff into the river. It was almost too much for the eye to comprehend. The noise was deafening. This time, we were closer to the waterfall than I wanted to be. And more rocks lay ahead. Suddenly, we were pulled into a glassy chute that slid over a nine-foot waterfall. At the bottom was what looked like a horizontal tornado of water.

As we slid over the falls, my abiding thought was disbelief. *My God, can this be happening?* But I knew that it was. Now, with an even tighter grip on the safety line and my head low (as if that would change anything), I felt the raft hit bottom. It waffled in on itself but quickly regained its shape, just in time to be sucked into the tornado's vortex. The next few seconds were a blur. We were completely at the mercy of the rapids. Suddenly, we were ejected to less angry waters. We had made it. We were through Lost Yak.

Adrenaline pumping wildly, I watched the others navigate the rapids, ready to help if needed. No need. Everyone made it through.

Next up was Lava South. Until Sobek explored the rapid in 1978, Lava Falls on the Colorado River was considered by many to be the toughest stretch of whitewater in the Americas. However, when guides who have run both rivers are forced to choose, most concede that Lava South is in a class by itself.

Our guides took a long scouting trip on Lava. When they returned, Mike briefed us on what to expect and what to do in case of trouble. After untying the last line that held our raft to shore, we pushed off.

Again, Stan's raft went first. We were right behind. Mike moved into the current after a signal that Stan was OK. Immediately, we were whacked by a wall of water, followed by another, and another—all from different directions. The raft was like a piece of balsa wood bouncing from crest to crest. At times, I thought we were out of control, but Mike was cool as he avoided a large group of boulders bisecting the river. My vague impression was that there were fewer rocks here than Lost Yak, but the rapids were worse. It was like being in a giant washing machine. Angry, raging rapids smashed into the rocks and each other.

Suddenly, we dropped into a deep hole. Mary screamed. Whiplash from the drop had banged her chin on the center frame of the raft. We'd find out later that she was bruised but OK.

Mike now aimed for a tongue of water beside the cliff to avoid one of Lava's unrunnable waterfalls. We hit the cliff and heard one of our back-up oars—always secured to the craft—snap like a stick. (Each raft has two extra oars secured to its sides.) Undistracted, Mike avoided another collision with the cliff, and suddenly we were heading into a welcome eddy of calm water. It was over. Hallelujah!

It was a rush to realize we'd made it through Lava South. It was like passing a big test. All of us were exhilarated, and the glow would last for days.

The next morning, we entered Royal Flush Canyon and ran four more exciting class four and five rapids. Ace, King, Queen, and, in particular, One-Eyed Jack rapids were wild and unpredictable. However, all rafts made it through without mishap.

As our trip wound down, we began to see workers on the rocky slope overlooking the river. They were operating bulldozers and trucks on a make-shift road for what was to be the first of a series of hydroelectric dams for the country. The dams had been proposed by a Chilean power company years earlier, and construction was underway despite opposition from environmental groups. The Natural Resources Defense Counsel contended that the dams were not necessary and would flood the ancestral lands of the Pehuenche Indians, still living in the upper Bío-Bío region. The power company and its supporters, however, stated that Chilé needed electricity to grow.

Our last day on the river was quiet. We rowed slowly to the riverside town of Santa Barbara, our take-out point, where we cleaned and deflated the rafts, loading them and other gear into a waiting truck. Everybody helped, except Judy, who had to sit it out with her foot elevated on her black bag.

We knew that there would be sights to see in Santiago and probably some meals with our new friends. But we also knew that the special quality of our days on the river would not happen again.

Norma O'Brien, the sales-lady from Chicago and a senior like us, announced loudly to no one in particular, "This was the wildest, most exciting thing I have ever done in my entire life! What a blast."

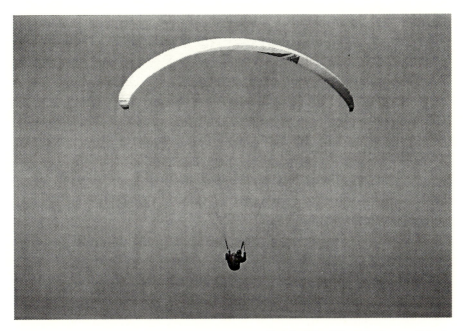

PARASAILING

In 1961, Pierre Lemoigne, a French inventor, had an idea. He decided to modify the traditional round parachute so it would ascend when towed by an automobile. He called it parascending, and it was developed to train soldiers to be parachutists. This was achieved by towing a "flyer"—in a modified parachute to a desired altitude and releasing him from the tow, an approach that proved considerably cheaper than getting him up in an airplane. In the same year of Lemoigne's invention, the Pioneer Parachute Company of Manchester, Connecticut, began manufacturing this design and marketed it under the trade name parascending.

Later that year, another variation of parascending was developed for recreational purposes. The participant, or "flyer," was towed not by a car, but by a boat, and that was called parasailing. The flyer usually started out standing on a beach, strapped into a body harness with an open parachute behind him.

The flyer would run along the beach with a helper running behind him, holding the open chute to prevent it from snagging. Offshore, the tow boat began lifting the flyer aloft to the desired altitude. To descend, the parasailor pulled down on the parachute's riser lines to maneuver the parachute and himself over a beach for a safe landing.

However, landings were then, and still are, when most accidents occur.

Commercial parasailing is still somewhat fragmented and unregulated, with some operators working independently without industry standards to guide them. Between 1985 and1995, an estimated 230 landing accidents occurred worldwide.

In the year 2000, for example, the Parasail Safety Council's list of parasailing accidents included the following:

*A California man suffered permanent nerve damage to his neck and back after a violent water landing.
*A Florida teenager fell through trees on shore after her parasail line snapped.
*A man's towline broke in high winds in Puerto Rico, causing him to hit the water at a high rate of speed. He was dragged across onshore rocks, receiving severe lacerations to his head and body.
*A parasailor in Clearwater Beach, Florida, was dragged to his death on the beach when the captain of the boat cut him loose during a violent wind storm.

According to the Parasail Safety Council, from 1990 to 2003 there were over 334 accidents; 68 resulting in serious injury and eleven in death in the United States. They have improved the equipment used in parasailing, and in 2004, no major accidents were reported.

I discovered parasailing by chance. I was in a restaurant in Orlando, Florida, working on an IBM task force that was exploring the possibility of an IBM-sponsored pavilion at Disneyworld. Four of us were having lunch at a table by several large windows. We were talking and looking out at the attractive lakefront beach populated by bathers.

Suddenly, a man in a bathing suit came into view. He seemed to be flying some fifty feet off the ground. He was sitting in a harness seat hooked to a billowing parachute that was connected by a towline to a speeding motorboat on the lake. As the boat pulled the parachute, it filled with air, keeping the parasailor aloft. It was an incredible sight, and I thought that it would be fun to do one day. The opportunity would come three years later.

In the spring of 1983, I was attending a three-day meeting for IBM in Miami when I learned about a parasail company that was offering rides for a fee in Fort Lauderdale, forty miles north of us. When our meeting was over, my IBM boss at the time, Cliff Jenks, and I decided to head north and take our first parasailing ride.

In Fort Lauderdale, we changed into bathing suits and headed directly for the beach, where we found the parasail company. If you could call it that. It appeared to be a four-man operation: two in a boat, and two on shore, one of whom seemed to be the owner. Darkly tanned, short, and overweight, the apparent owner was barking orders to his associates to un-harness a young woman who had just come in from her parasail ride. He wore shorts, sandals, sunglasses, and a faded Boston Red Sox cap. He also had on a bright red T-shirt emblazoned with the words: "Parasail Adventures, Inc." Cliff and I introduced ourselves to him (we'll call him Milton) and said we wanted to parasail.

"Wind's getting nasty," Milton said with a strong Boston accent. "Could be a problem."

As he continued working on the parachute that had just come in, he casually looked over at Cliff and said slowly, "You can probably go." Without missing a beat, he looked at me and said—almost dismissively—I thought, "But you're too light."

"I've wanted to do this for a long time," I whined. "Might be the only chance I have."

"Hard to get the chute down over fifteen knots," he said. "Close to that now."

Seeing my disappointment, he relented.

"OK," he said, "tell you what—let's put your friend up now, and if the wind eases up by the time he's back, *maybe* we can get you up. That's all I can promise."

"OK," I said, happy for any encouragement.

Milton gave Cliff a life jacket to put on and strapped him into a sturdy nylon harness seat that connected to the parachute. I watched begrudgingly as Cliff was briefed by Milton on what to do when he was aloft. Sixty feet from shore, Milton's motorboat was idling in the water. Both boatmen were eager to get going.

Milton picked up Cliff's parachute from the sandy beach and carefully straightened the shroud lines so they wouldn't snag on anything. He asked Cliff if he was ready (he was), and Milton signaled his crew in the boat. The boat immediately roared to life and sliced through the ocean parallel to the shore. The tow rope went taut, and the parachute suddenly popped open.

Milton shouted at Cliff, "OK, start running!!" Cliff ran along the beach in the same direction that the boat was heading. Milton ran behind Cliff, holding the parachute at waist level so it could inflate more easily. Within seconds, Cliff's parachute filled with air and began to rise gracefully over the beach, heading for a target altitude of 250 feet.

Within minutes, Cliff was flying through the air. It was quite a sight.

I sat on the beach for about half an hour, watching and waiting for his return. I thought the wind had lessened, but it was hard to tell.

Then I saw Cliff's parachute approaching in a slow descent. From where I sat, his chute looked fine. I watched Milton's men in the boat slowly winch Cliff and his parachute lower and lower until they found a spot on the beach to let him land, well beyond the bathers. Milton and one of his employees positioned themselves to grab a second line, called the "drag line," that hung loosely from the bottom of Cliff's seat. In less than a minute, Milton and his co-worker were able to grab the line and pull Cliff safely down to a soft landing on the sand. He had a big grin on his face when he saw me.

"Great!" he told me. "One heck of a ride."

Milton quickly helped him out of his harness. As I walked over, Cliff was gesturing and smiling as he described his flight to Milton. Before I could say a word, Milton looked over at me and barked, "Still want to go up?"

"Of course!" I said.

"The wind's backed off a bit," he said, "Might not last long, though, so let's get going!"

He turned sharply, picked up Cliff's discarded chute, and once again began to straighten the shroud lines.

Hey! Looks like I'm finally going to parasail, I thought. The classic quotation, "Be careful of what you wish for" also came to mind.

Milton put me in the harness and soon I was ready, waiting for the boat to start. As he had for Cliff, Milton signaled the boat, and then shouted at me, "Start running!"

I did so, and, within seconds, I could hear and feel the parachute behind me filling with air, and then "Whoops!" it began to rise—and me with it. Within no more than five minutes, it seemed, I had leveled out at 250 feet above the Atlantic Ocean.

Everything was happening so fast, it was a bit scary. Here I was sitting in this dinky little seat way up in the air. I felt very vulnerable. Slowly, I looked down at my all-important, tow line—my umbilical cord, as it were. It connected me to the boat below me that, at the moment, looked as small as a credit card.

In fact, everything looked small. Other boats below seemed to be moving in slow motion, their white wakes gracefully etching the blue sea. People on the beach were virtual specks, hardly moving, or so it seemed.

To lighten up and relax, I adopted some gallows humor by talking loudly to myself: "The most important safety rule on this ride is: Do Not Fall Out Of Your Seat!"

I knew that my first order of business was to sit up straight, because I was scrunched into one side of the seat. Slowly I began to inch my body closer to the center. When I got there—without anything bad happening—I felt good about my meager accomplishment.

Now I began to loosen up. After all, there was so much to see, so much to take in. But first, I wanted to check essentials—like my parachute because, without that, I was seafood. Looking up at it, I shouted aloud, "Yes!" It was still there, full of air, and doing its job. Next, I looked down at the tow boat, my other lifeline. All seemed well, and I waved to the two men mouthing the words, "Hey guys, we're going to have a safe trip. Right?"

They waved back. So far, so good, I thought.

Gazing down at the beach again, I was fascinated by how people looked from this height I tried to figure out what they were doing. Some were swimming, but most were spread out on the sand or strolling on the beach. *And look at that*, I thought, *a bunch of girls waving at me.* I waved back and mouthed, "Hi girls, how ya' doing'?"

After awhile, I noticed that my tow boat was making a slow, lazy turn for its return trip. I looked straight down at the circle of white water created by the boat's wake. I estimated the entire ride to be about forty-five minutes. Distance covered: perhaps a mile.

All my fear had evaporated, and I was feeling good. I checked my parachute and how the harness hooked into the seat. But I most enjoyed watching people on the beach. I'd try to focus on one person until I could figure out what he or she was doing. I could make out a child filling his pail with sand, a woman applying sun-tan lotion, a young boy diving into the surf. I waved at people and occasionally get a wave back.

I was now approaching my landing site on the beach, not far from where I had lifted off. I noticed that the wind was picking up.

The usual procedure for a parasail landing is for the tow boat to come as close to shore as possible but still be beyond the bathers so that the flyer ends up hovering over the sandy beach. When the tow boat reaches its desired position, the crew signals the flyer to pull down on his "riser" lines (on each side of him). That makes the flyer's parachute slowly deflate by squeezing air out from under its canopy. The more air removed, the lower the parachute descends. At the same time, the ocean's winds push the parachute toward shore for a soft landing.

Looking down, I could see that my tow boat had stopped at a spot safely beyond the swimmers. The boatman signaled me to pull down my riser lines, which I did. Predictably the parachute dropped lower. However, it didn't drop as quickly as I had expected.

The winds *were* stronger.

I was directly over the beach but still too high for the crew to reach the drag line. Bobbing in the wind, I watched Milton and one of his men, directly below me, jumping for the rope. Once again they shouted at me to pull on the riser lines. I did, but this time the wind resisted almost all my efforts. I had descended only ten feet or so. I was still thirty feet off the ground.

And the wind was getting stronger.

I noticed that some of the bathers were gathering to watch the "show." I continued to pull hard on my riser lines but could drop only a foot or two at best. I was still twenty-five feet off the ground, and the wind was now whipping my chute in several directions. I was becoming concerned.

I could tell that Milton and his assistants were frustrated, angry, and tired. They simply couldn't reach the elusive drag line swinging defiantly under my seat. It seemed as if an air pocket was trapped in the parachute, holding it captive in the wind.

The crowd had grown to sixty or seventy people, mostly bathers who were watching the drama play out. The mood almost seemed festive. People were eating hot dogs and drinking beer, smiling and laughing. It was like a circus. One geezer yelled to his geezerette friend and beckoned. "Shirley, come over here and check this out. You can swim later."

A woman held a baby under her arm and a little boy with her other hand. When the boy tried to break away, his mother slapped him. He fell crying to the sand. *Play within a play*, I thought as I watched helplessly. Most people just stood and stared, shouting occasional support for Milton and his now harried assistant whenever either of them came close to grabbing the line.

I was feeling like a performer on display, and my hands were raw from pulling on the lines.

Then, another disquieting development: From my lofty perch, I had a panoramic view of not only the beach and people in front of me, but now—because of the increased winds—I could also see the busy road traffic in back of me. A major thoroughfare butted up to the beach. As long as the wind blew vertically, our parachute problem could be contained. But now, with the wind changing direction, the parachute's path was no longer predictable. If the wind pushed the parachute into that traffic, the problem would be serious.

With his knowledge of the area, Milton must have known what could happen. He shouted more angrily and desperately at me, "Pull the riser lines again! Pull harder. Keep pulling! Keep pulling!"

As I swung in my seat, I remembered Milton's earlier concern about my weight. He was absolutely right, of course. I was too light. Perhaps a heavier person wouldn't be having this problem. I also wondered, as I gazed down at his sweating head, what he was thinking now. His Red Sox cap had fallen off and was being thoroughly stomped into the sand by the two men.

Then, suddenly, a break.

For one, brief moment, the wind slowed, and I reacted by pulling even harder than before. A corner of the chute sagged. It drooped for no more than a second or two, but it was long enough for Milton's employee to grab the line. Milton grabbed on as well, and the two men finally conquered the wind and dragged me back to earth.

The show was over, and our impromptu audience broke into applause, cheers, and whistles. Instinctively, I joined them by clapping my hands for all of them and their patience.

Years later, I still get a few questions about my experience, usually ending with, "Would you ever go parasailing again?"

To which I reply, "I don't think so."

Crossing the Dudh Kosi Bridge

TREKKING in NEPAL

Trekking down a narrow trail from Namché Bazaar, we could see a small caravan of people and yaks coming toward us. We heard a noisy mix of English and Nepali above the rhythmic clanging of yak bells. It was a group of about ten people and two yaks. As they approached, we thought about how best to share the trail when our groups converged. One side of the trail was a mountain wall and the other, a rocky ledge with a fifteen-foot drop.

"Judy," Nima said sharply. "Stand over here! Near the wall."

"I'm OK," she said. "I've got a good hold of this tree trunk."

The enormous yak leading the procession plodded slowly toward us. I was flat against the mountain wall, but Judy—on the other side—was still too close to the edge, I thought. But it was too late now to change positions.

As the yak began to pass between us, it slowed down and inexplicably started to force Judy off the ledge with its sheer bulk. Knowing how mean-spirited yaks can be, Nima nimbly jumped in front of the animal, grabbing Judy's arm as he did. He pulled her farther down the trail so they could cross to the safety of the rock wall.

It was a brief but scary moment.

Judy and I were in the ancient Kingdom of Nepal, trekking in the Himalayas with our guide, Nima, and two porters. We were there to see Mount Everest, the highest mountain in the world. We also wanted to see Nepal, a country of myth and mystery nestled between the borders of India and Tibet. Both of us enjoyed trekking, and the idea of doing it in such a legendary place—changed little over the millennia—was exciting.

Nepal has been open to tourists since 1951. It is a country of 56.8 million square miles—about the size of the state of Michigan. The country has a rectangular shape, about five hundred miles from west to east and one hundred miles from north to south. Nepal is also home to two of the world's great religions, Buddhism and Hinduism. Nepal has a population of twenty-one million people, most of whom work as farmers.

We had signed up with. Mt. Travel-Sobek for the tour company's Everest Adventure, a thirteen-day trip. It was scheduled for October, when the weather is usually cool and the skies clear.

However, temperatures can vary from ninety degrees Fahrenheit to below freezing at night.

Our trip had been a long one, with layovers in Seattle, Tokyo, and Bangkok before finally landing in Katmandu, Nepal's capital. There, a Mt.Travel representative met us and took us to the Malla Hotel, where we were to stay two nights. We planned to spend a full day sightseeing in Katmandu.

Nepal is thirteen and a half hours ahead of the United States' Pacific time zone. At noon on January 1 in California, it's 1:30 AM on January 2 in Nepal. We lost a day crossing the International Date Line on our way to Nepal and would gain it back on our return home.

We got to our room in Katmandu after 9:00 PM, and we were bushed. We planned to unpack our luggage and get some sleep so we'd be fresh the next day. We had hardly finished unpacking when there was a loud knock at the door. I opened it to see a very excited older Nepalese gentleman. He introduced himself as J.P. Lama, an employee for Mt. Travel. He told us that he was responsible for our flight to the Lukla Airport—first stop on our Himalayan trek.

"Your flight is changed," he announced excitedly. "We must go tomorrow, not day after. We go tomorrow! Early, 6:00 AM!" We told him that we had just gotten in and hadn't slept in twenty-four hours, but he just repeated his mantra, "We must go tomorrow at 6:00 AM!"

So we agreed to go the next morning at 6:00 AM.

The next morning at the Royal Nepal Airport was an experience. The small terminal was packed with people, mostly Nepalese. J.P. helped us get our luggage checked in. We would fly on a two-engine Twin-Otter that seated nineteen people. All seats were taken. The plane took off smoothly, and Judy and I settled down to relax. But that was not to be. Fifteen minutes into the flight, the captain's voice came over the intercom.

"Unfortunately, we are experiencing visibility problems," he said. "We must fly back to Katmandu. We will try tomorrow."

We had been warned that, because of unpredictable weather, the flight to Lukla was unreliable. For that reason, Mt. Travel routinely adds an extra day to Nepal itineraries.

We returned to the hotel and our original plan to see Katmandu. It was Sunday, and we discovered that we could attend ten o'clock Mass at St. Xavier's Catholic Church. We hired a cab to take us there and pick us up an hour later.

St. Xavier's Church turned out to be essentially a large room with a modest altar. There were no chairs, and it was crowded with people sitting on the floor with their legs crossed in Buddhist fashion. We entered and did the same.

Except for the priest, who, surprisingly, was American, we were the only westerners. The service was in Nepalese but otherwise no different from what we were accustomed to in the United States, so we felt comfortable. The Nepali people were very friendly, something we would experience often in the days ahead.

After Mass, Judy and I talked to the tall, Irish priest, who told us he had been there for six years and loved the people and his mission. He was from Boston, Massachusetts, where I went to school. Of course I had to ask him about the Red Sox and the "curse of the Bambino."

"Say a prayer for them, Father." I said jokingly. Without missing a beat, he replied, "I have, but it hasn't worked yet."

Katmandu is a bustling city of half a million people. In addition to taxis, there were bicycles, electric scooters, rickshaws, automobiles, buses (always loaded with people), and trucks, all competing for space on the crowded roads. Pungent odors of fruit, incense, spices, and vehicle exhaust permeated the air. Vendors sold fruits and vegetables from small stands and yelled at the kids and cows that tried to eat them. We heard children and crying babies everywhere.

The following morning at the airport, we tried again. This time, Judy and I had seats on the left side of the aircraft directly behind the pilots. Our plane took off without incident. Well into the flight, we had a spectacular view of the Himalayas. We could see their majestic, snow-laden peaks against a cold, blue sky and framed from below by clouds.

After thirty minutes, I spotted Lukla Airport through the pilot's windshield. It was a tiny airfield, carved out of steep mountain rock above the Dudh Kosi River, which our trek was to parallel.

We had been warned by J.P. that, because of the mountains and the size of the airfield, landings had to be perfect or we'd fly right back to Katmandu. Once a pilot committed to land, he had to land. He didn't have the luxury of taking another pass if he didn't like what he saw.

I could see through the window a crowd of people standing around the perimeter of the airfield waiting for us to come in. Some of them, I thought, were likely waiting for people on our plane, while others were planning to travel to Katmandu on our plane. I was told later that most of them were probably from Lukla and just curious to see the new arrivals.

I couldn't help but notice that our pilot kept peering at what looked like a cocktail napkin attached to his window visor. He'd take it down, look at it for a moment, talk to the co-pilot, and then put it back on the visor. I saw that the day's date and a few numbers were written on the napkin in ink.

Then I realized that the numbers corresponded to our departure and arrival times. I was looking at the captain's *flight plan*. On the back of a cocktail napkin? I smiled and mumbled to myself, "So what were you expecting—American Airlines?"

We landed, literally rolling up the small hill at the end of the runway. The hill was clearly there to slow or stop an aircraft in case of a problem.

Whatever works! I thought.

After landing, things really got frenetic. We went looking for our luggage. The people on the ground who were heading back to Katmandu were already queued up to get on board the aircraft.

I saw a short man with a big smile and dark, tousled hair approaching me. There were two boys behind him. He politely asked: "Mr. and Mrs. Donald Mac Isaac?"

"That's us," I said.

Slowly, he said: "I am Nima Wongohhu Sherpa, your Sidar (guide). I am happy to meet you. These are our porters, Chaapte and Sundra. They are hard workers."

Nima was in his early thirties, wiry and thin, without a gram of fat on him. The boys were young—fourteen or fifteen and also thin. They spoke little English and appeared shy.

Chaapte, Nima, and Sundra

"I'm Don," I said, "and this is my wife, Judy. We are very happy to meet you, Nima, and your porters." I nodded to the porters. "Wasn't there another couple on this trip?" I asked.

"Not coming," Nima said. "They cancel last week. It's just you and your wife."

Calendar conflicts seemed to be the major reason.

Now we were learning that the last two people had cancelled, and I wasn't sure that I liked that. After all, it's nice to have other people to talk to in a shared adventure.

Yet, on the other hand, I thought, this would be like having our own personal staff, and that didn't sound bad either. (It wouldn't take long for us to realize that we had a good deal.)

As the boys grabbed our luggage and we put on our daypacks, Nima pointed with his finger and said, "We go this way to Sherpa guide lodge."

Sherpa guide lodges are located throughout the Himalayas and used by many trekkers—especially amateurs like us. With no inside plumbing and only four hours of electricity in the evening, they are far from luxurious—but they sure beat a sleeping bag in the sub-zero night temperatures.

And they are clean. There are no motor vehicles in the hamlet of Lukla. We left the airport and walked toward a cluster of buildings half a mile away. The cobblestone road was narrow and snaked through town. We saw people walking and children playing in the street. Dogs barked at no one in particular, and chickens clucked imperiously.

I'll never forget one little girl—about three years old, with sad eyes. She was sitting on a wooden bench, holding a brick in her lap, much like any little girl her age might hold a doll. She stared at us unblinkingly as we walked by.

Little girl with a brick

A modest sign on a small, weathered building asserted itself to be the Paradise Hotel, located near the air strip. Nima took us in for a cup of tea while he and his "crew" assembled our luggage and their necessities for the trek. We were greeted at the lodge by a fourteen-year-old Chinese boy who spoke some English. He said his name was "F.B.," and it was his job was to wait on trekkers (like us) on their way to the mountains. He served us tea, and we had a chance to talk to him. He told us that both his parents were killed in Communist China years earlier. He was taken into a Christian missionary school, where he learned English and how to read and write. After two years, he told us, he decided to leave China and look for opportunities elsewhere.

He said he enjoyed reading, and we talked about books. I mentioned a few titles, asking if he'd like to read them. He said he would. (I mailed them to him after we got home.) As I think back on our conversation, I am sure that F.B. did well. He had a raw, basic intelligence and "street smarts" far beyond his years. A tough combination to beat in any country.

After lunch, Nima briefed us on what to expect that afternoon and the days to follow. Our immediate destination was Phakding (Fake-DING), four hours away.

Lukla was at 9,200 feet and Phakding at 8,875 feet, and we would actually be descending on the trail for periods of time.

"That will help you get used to altitude," Nima said with a smile. "Then tomorrow we practice climb to Buddhist monastery, high up mountain.

"This gets you ready for Namche Bazaar, which is 11,300 feet. You will be tired next day," Nima continued. "After Namche Bazaar, we climb higher so you can see Everest. Then, we come back down the mountain here to Lukla."

It felt good the next day to finally get on the trail—especially one that's been used for centuries. Soon we were trekking through forests, fields, and villages. We saw many people. Nima led the way with an effortless gait. Judy and I followed, with our porters right behind.

There was beauty everywhere. We were particularly impressed by the elaborate rice terraces sculpted anywhere there was space to put them. They were on the tops and sides of mountains as well as in the valleys.

The dictionary defines a trek as a journey or trip that involves difficulty or hardship. Having hiked and rock-climbed, I'd say that's a fair description. Certainly rock-climbing is altogether different, in that the climb is technical on a rock mountain and often requires ropes, pitons, caribiners, and the like.

While trekking may seem the easier endeavor, it depends on the trek. I suspect that anyone trekking ten or fifteen miles in one day up several thousand feet would not describe it as easy.

The weather couldn't have been better—about sixty degrees Fahrenheit. Our trail was far from lonely. Since it is one of the main routes to Mount Everest, we saw many expedition members going to or coming from base camp. Sherpas carried astonishingly large loads, and the yaks carried the heaviest weights, like oxygen tanks, aluminum ladders, and food. Maybe that's why yaks always seem grumpy.

It was fascinating to see real expeditions of climbers heading for Mount Everest—something that Judy and I had seen only on television.

Trekking in Nepal can be rigorous, and never was that more evident than when we had to cross the bridges of the Dudh Kosi River (River of Milk). We would cross the river not once but several times in a day—each way—going up the trail and coming back.

Bridge spans ranged from forty to one hundred feet, depending on the width of the river: The wider the chasm, the longer the bridge.

Bridge construction in Nepal has been dictated by the mountainous terrain. When efforts to develop trails on one side of the river were thwarted by rock, the Nepalese built bridges to the other side, the only alternative.

Most of the bridges were three or four feet wide and made of wood planking, with occasional planks missing. Steel cables on each side of the bridge held up a metal mesh fence that prevented trekkers like us from falling into the river. Nonetheless, each crossing was an adventure. We never knew whom or what we would encounter.

The rules were simple. Whoever got to the bridge first crossed first. There was one exception that everyone observed: Yaks always had the right of way.

The first bridge we encountered was about thirty feet above the churning river and spanned fifty feet bank to bank. When we stepped on the bridge, the first thing we felt was the swaying.

There wasn't a lot of movement—just enough to make sure that we paid attention to what we were doing.

Like a veteran ballet dancer, Nima hardly broke stride as he smoothly walked over the aging span to the other side. Turning around, he looked back at me and beckoned.

"OK, Don. You come!"

I stepped onto the bridge and gripped a cable. I watched carefully for holes in the planking as I slowly made my way to the other side.

When I got there, I waved to Judy to join Nima and me. She crossed the span as if she had been doing it for years.

After five bridges, I thought I had it down pretty well. But then came the sixth bridge.

As was my pattern, I confidently stepped on the bridge, took a quick look to the other side, saw no one coming, and then began looking for the ubiquitous holes in the planking.

I should have set my gaze a tad higher. Suddenly I heard someone yelling at me from the other side.

I glanced up to see a very large, flint-eyed yak on the bridge coming directly toward me. Behind the animal, its apparent owner was waving his arms and shouting words at me that didn't sound friendly.

The problem was apparent. There wasn't enough room on the bridge to pass each other, and something had to give. The enormous animal (No wonder there are holes in the planking.) was now within twenty feet of me and showed no signs of stopping. And now the bridge was swaying more than what I had gotten used to.

I quickly got the message and made a 180-degree course correction to get the hell off the bridge. In Nepal one does not argue with yaks.

At 5:00 PM we reached the Sherpa guide lodge in Phakding. We had been climbing close to four hours and were tired and hungry. The lodge was a modest, two-story building that accommodated up to sixteen people in eight double rooms.

Despite our fatigue, we felt good about the day. We had kept up with Nima at the pace he set without problems, and we were doing what we had come halfway around the world to do: trekking in Nepal.

Our comfortable second-floor room had two single beds, a closet, and a small table. Our window had a stunning view of the mountains, which literally surrounded us. We collapsed on our beds and must have fallen asleep because a sharp knock on the door woke us.

"Dinner ready!" Nima yelled cheerfully.

As we walked downstairs, we could smell the welcome aroma of hot chicken, potatoes, pasta, and tea.

We had dinner and spent the evening around an indoor fireplace. Nima and the porters entertained us with a few short dances and songs of their boyhood.

The "Nima Trio," as we dubbed them, never made it through one song without "breaking up" in quick laughter. Their infectious laughter only made the songs more endearing.

At six o'clock we were up for a breakfast of orange juice, American corn flakes, toast with jam, and tea. We ate heartily, knowing that we had a rigorous trek en route to the Buddhist monastery. The trek to the monastery, at ten thousand feet, would be our warm-up for Namche Bazaar the following day.

The mountainous scenery was spectacular. We climbed up an ancient trail. At close to ten thousand feet, Judy mentioned a headache. Never a complainer, she looked flushed and was breathing rapidly. By the time we reached the monastery, she wasn't any better and had to sit down.

She had never been at this altitude before, and I was concerned. I spoke to Nima who said: "We'll go down soon, but first she should rest a while, drink water, and eat food."

Half an hour later, Judy said, "I think the food helped. I'm feeling better."

We were in Sagarmatha National Park and over the next few days would be heading into the world's highest mountain range. The Himalaya begins where other mountain ranges leave off. Everest base camp, for example, is at 6,402 feet, higher than the highest peak in Europe.

Later, we would learn at a tiny hospital in Khunde, a village on our trek route, that one's body can acclimatize to these altitudes only if given enough time to do so. Trekking must be done at a slow pace, or, as the Nepalis say "Bis-ta-rai!" Being in a hurry in the Himalaya can be deadly. If you fail to acclimatize, you may develop Acute Mountain Sickness (AMS), which can occur at any altitude over two thousand feet. Early symptoms are headaches, extreme fatigue, and loss of appetite. AMS results in fluid accumulating in parts of the body where it can be life-threatening, as in the brain (cerebral edema) or lungs (pulmonary edema) or both. In Nepal, one in every one thousand trekkers dies from AMS.

Someone suffering from AMS may not think clearly and has to be forced to descend (as I had to on my first Kilimanjaro climb). A person should not go beyond the altitude at which the symptoms began. It appeared that Judy had experienced the early stages of AMS. Fortunately, however, the longer she rested, the better she felt.

The Buddhist monastery was small—about thirty by forty feet, colorful, and perched on a rocky ledge ten thousand feet in the air. Two large doors were open to reveal a modest altar bedecked with lighted candles on several tiers. There were six pews, three on each side of an altar, where people could sit and pray. As we rested outside, we saw individuals and families from the area and beyond come to pay homage to Buddha. Most worshippers knelt or stood quietly before the icons on the altar, and most of them put money into a basket for the only lama who lived at the monastery.

Nima paid homage by praying before the altar. Judy and I did also to show our respect, and we left a contribution.

We were coming out of the monastery when we saw the local lama coming up the trail. He was old and wiry and well over six feet tall. He wore a long, weathered cotton tunic that covered most of his body except for his feet, which were adorned with an old pair of green Nike, high-top sneakers.

I asked Nima how the lama could get by so far from civilization.

"People on mountain bring him food and money all the time. He is never hungry," Nima said matter-of-factly. "He walks to Namche Bazaar or Lukla for medicine, clothes, and other things he needs."

Our return trip to Phakding was easier for Judy, who had regained most of her energy. Her headache was better, but we knew that she would need a good night's sleep and that we would have to go a little slower on the climb the next day to Namche Bazaar.

When we awoke the next morning, Judy and I felt great. She had slept like a stone and seemed to be revived and ready for our six-to seven-hour trek to Namche Bazaar.

We ate a big breakfast and were on the trail by seven o'clock. The weather was overcast, but the skies gradually cleared.

We trekked through blue pine forests, terraced fields, and a number of small villages. In many of the villages, we passed *mani* walls—sacred places where Buddhist prayers are carved in rock. Religious tradition required that we walk around them in a clockwise manner, which we all did.

Looming above us in the distance was Khumbila (18,800 feet), the sacred peak of the Sherpa people and sentinel of the spiritual and geographic heart of the Khumbu region. Khumbila remains unclimbed (sacred peaks may not be climbed) and is the "protector" deity of Tibetan Buddhists.

We continued through the hamlet of Jorsdale, the official entrance to the Sagarmatha (Mount Everest) National Park, established in 1976. This was the first national park in the Himalaya to protect an area of great environmental, religious, and cultural importance.

It was noon, and we had been climbing for over four hours. When Nima said we'd have lunch here, we were ready. Nima and I went into a small teahouse on the main street and bought some cooked chicken, rice, and bottled water.

We ate our meal at an outdoor picnic table in front of the teahouse and watched two Nepalis building a small house nearby. The activity and noise was constant as they hammered boards and mixed cement, even as children played around them. All their materials had to be carried in by the people by the people or yaks.

There are no vehicles on the mountains, but many trekkers were also going up and down the trail. Many stopped at the teahouse for food.

After lunch, we crossed a much larger bridge than the others. It had been engineered and built by the Swiss many years earlier. At one thousand feet above the river, it was the highest bridge that we had crossed. I took a photo of it from the ground because it was so impressive. It felt sturdy and safe when we crossed it.

Next we had to climb a switchback trail to Namche Bazaar. The trek was getting tougher, and I began to get cramps that later developed into the "trots." For a while, I saw every bush and boulder as a potential lavatory.

The trek was tiring. We were moving at a slower pace than the previous day, trying to avoid a return of Judy's headaches. It seemed to be helping. However, it was now getting dark, and we were an hour off our arrival schedule.

Just as the sun was about to set, Nima, who was well ahead of us, turned around at the crest of a hill and with a broad smile yelled back to us, "Namché Bazaar!" He had climbed to the bazaar over one thousand times.

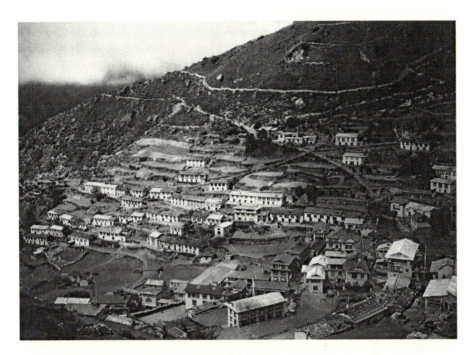

Namché Bazaar

I called back to Judy, "Hey Jude, look: Shangri-La!" (Nepal was the model for Shangri-La in James Hilton's book, *Lost Horizon.*) Namché Bazaar looked like a small jewel sitting on top of a mountain. It was a prosperous market town of two thousand people and the local center for trading and supplies.

The town has numerous homes, trekkers' inns, shops, and a small monastery and is beautifully situated in a terraced, natural amphitheater facing the hanging glacier below Kwangde (19,865 feet). The town is surrounded by prayer flags of every color. The sight revived our sagging spirits.

To make the moment even more magical, the lights came on in town—almost on cue—as we reached the crest. It was like seeing a twinkling little village from an airplane. But we weren't in an airplane. We were standing in one of the most remote spots in the world, where logic would suggest that there should be *no* town.

Electricity was introduced to Namché Bazaar in 1983, when a UNESCO-sponsored hydroelectric plant located below the village began operating. As in Phakding, electricity would come on at 6:00 PM and go off at 10:00 PM.

We all had a quicker step as we approached the town. As before, we were to stay at a Sherpa guide lodge overnight before going to see Mount Everest the next day. When we reached the lodge, I remembered that I was tired. Judy was also, but the headache had eased. The slower pace had made the difference, we concluded, even though we were at 11,300 feet, the highest altitude she'd ever reached.

After dinner, Judy and I were ready for some serious sleep. The day had caught up with us, and we had to make our apologies to Nima and the porters—who were ready to party and sing again as they did in Phakding. However, we knew that this wasn't the first time their clients were "sucking air" in Namché Bazaar.

And wouldn't you know, about 3:00 AM, with temperatures hovering around five degrees Fahrenheit, I had to get out of my warm bed to visit the local outhouse, or "thunder box," as Nima called it.

Trying to find a small outhouse thirty yards away from the lodge on the darkest night of my life was daunting. Even with my headlamp on, I couldn't find it. So, mumbling some appropriate imprecation, I did my duty where I was.

Turning around to make my way back to the lodge, I then discovered that I couldn't find the lodge. *How do you lose a lodge?* I asked myself. Everything was pitch black. There were no stars, no moon, no reference points. *Some explorer I am*, I thought. *Not only can't I find the outhouse, I can't even find the in-house.*

What I didn't realize at the time was that at high altitude, it's easy to become disoriented—especially at night—with less blood to the brain causing impaired judgment.

I thought about yelling for help but decided it was too embarrassing. My eyes finally began to adjust to the gloom. Then I saw something big and black. The lodge!

Hooray! I muttered to myself. With my headlamp bobbing light on the pathway, I finally found the lodge door from which I had come. At last, after what seemed like an eternity, I was back in a warm bed. All was well with the world.

The next morning, we were again up at six o'clock and quickly consumed a big breakfast. After all, this was the day when we would see Mount Everest. We had to be at a viewing spot no later than 10:00 AM, before clouds obscured the view of the mountain.

Back on the trail, we trekked another seven hundred feet to the Sagarmantha National Park and visited the museum that was given to the Nepalese people by Sir. Edmund Hillary. Hillary was the first person to climb Mount Everest, in 1953. We saw the original equipment that he and his Nepalese guide, Norgay Tensing, used in their climb—equipment considered primitive by today's standards.

Nima mentioned that Sir Edmund had also built and donated many schools, hospitals, and clinics to the Nepalese people. He is much loved by the people of the country.

Mount Everest was named for Sir George Everest (1790-1866), a British surveyor general of India. Tibetans call it Chomolunga. Nepalese call it Sagarmantha. The first American to reach the summit was Jim Whittaker, on May 1, 1963, accompanied by his Nepalese guide, Nawang Gombu.

Nima now led us to a vantage point where we could see Mount Everest, mother of all mountains, at 29,028 feet. Also in view was Lhotse at 27,890 feet; Nuptse at 25,580 feet; and, perhaps the most beautiful of all Nepal's mountains, Aba Dablam at 22,490 feet.

Judy in front of Mount Everest

Unlike the Matterhorn, with its awesome, dramatic peak, Everest has no such beautiful peak. But when I realized that I was looking at the tallest mountain in the world, I felt privileged to see it. I stared at Everest, thinking of it almost as a giant Buddha sitting in massive serenity, surrounded by its acolyte mountains.

The following day we went to Namché Bazaar so Judy could do some shopping. Nepalese music played in the background and multi-colored religious flags flew at the bazaar, a conglomerate of shops and booths selling everything from food to jewelry to clothing. There were also some interesting works of art, including intricate wood carvings. Unfortunately (or fortunately, as the case may be) we did not have much room in our bags.

Saturday is the big day at Namché, the economic hub of the region. People from miles around bring their produce and livestock to sell at the market. We met many of them on a crowded trail the next day as we headed south to Phakding.

We were on trail by 7:00 AM Saturday, and it was much easier going down than up. Judy and I also felt better. However, it was still a slow descent, made slower by people heading for Namché Bazaar.

In addition to the Nepalis, we saw a number of European and American trekkers. During rest stops, we talked to people from Dallas, Boston, and Germany, most of them younger than us. There were a few older Europeans, which didn't surprise us since trekking and hiking are so popular in Europe. I talked to and envied a writer from Colorado. He was about forty years old and heading for Mount Everest Base Camp at 18,188 feet to do a story about his experience.

We reached Phakding by mid-afternoon, and it was nice to see the familiar Sherpa lodge. We took a nap and were awakened later by the sound of women's voices downstairs. For the first time on our trip, we had company.

At dinner we met them—five friends from California who would be trekking together up to Namche Bazaar in the morning. They were bright, interesting professionals in their early forties. They had decided together a year earlier that they needed a little adventure in their lives. They'd done a lot of climbing in the California Sierras and were not novices. They had left their husbands and companions at home to take care of whomever and whatever. This was their time. Judging by the brief visit we had with them and the fun at dinner, I think they were ready for a good time.

The next morning after breakfast, we said goodbye to the ladies as they departed north to Namche and we went south to Lukla.

We trekked back to Lukla and checked in at the Sherpa lodge to prepare for our flight back to Katmandu. Nima and I sat down after lunch, and we offered gratuities for him and his porters. He seemed pleased, as was I, with the warm, comfortable relationship that had developed between him, his porters, and us during the past week. Nima would have a two-day trek to get back to his home and family. We exchanged farewells with promises to correspond.

In the morning, there were about thirty of us anxiously waiting at the small airfield for one of the two flights scheduled back to Katmandu. Because of past disappointments, none of us felt all that confident about the flight getting off the ground on time. But we were hopeful.

While waiting for the planes, a group of young, energetic Italian trekkers were having a fine time teasing each other and running around the airfield. Judy and I also met four young people (two men and two women) who were in the Peace Corps. They had been teaching in Nepal for over a year and were going back to Katmandu for reassignment. Both Judy and I were impressed, thinking that they were superb representatives of our country.

After a couple of hours, we heard the reassuring sound of a plane approaching and we all cheered. The plane landed without incident and, after the incoming passengers got off, the Italian contingent and others noisily boarded the aircraft. The pilot told us that the second plane that we were waiting for would arrive shortly and not to worry.

Our "Hail Mary" Take off

I pulled out my camera to get a shot of the first plane taxiing for takeoff. In my many years of flying, I had never seen such a short runway as the one at Lukla. It appeared shorter than the length of a football field and, at the end of it, was a cliff that dropped away into a chasm. It was obvious that the plane's wheels had better be off the ground before reaching the edge. However, we were told that Nepalese pilots were very good and had an excellent safety record.

The Twin Otter, perched on the little hill, gunned its motors and seemed to be thrust by a sling-shot toward the precipice. I was taking photos of the action as fast as my finger could move the shutter. Just seconds before the plane reached the critical point, the pilot pulled back, and the plane ascended, but not before making a little dip—eliciting gasps from some of us watching.

Sure enough, the second plane showed up about half an hour later, and we had a safe, relaxed flight back to Katmandu.

Looking at our photos some months later after we were home, we could clearly see the dip when the airplane literally flew off the cliff. Judy dubbed it our "Hail Mary flight."

After the trip, several people asked us "Why would you want to go to Nepal?"

I read an old Sanskrit poem in Katmandu that answered the question better than we ever could: "In a hundred ages of the Gods, I could not tell you of all the glories of the Himalaya."

And you know what? Neither could we.

Kingston, NY Freeman photo by Keith Hitlin

FLYING in an OPEN COCKPIT BIPLANE

When I was a kid, my mother took me to see *The Dawn Patrol*, a black and white movie starring the swashbuckling actors Errol Flynn and David Niven. The film was about World War I fighter pilots, who flew in flimsy, open-cockpit airplanes. I was riveted by the danger that they always seemed to be in, especially the dog fights. (I'd always applaud when the bad guy was shot down.)

At the time, I remember wondering what it would be like to fly in such an airplane one day. Even then, I knew it was unlikely I would get the chance.

Many years later, in 1964, I was a writer working for IBM in Kingston, New York, when the company announced its System

360—a new family of computers that would revolutionize the computer industry. Customers were offered more choices in power, size, and flexibility. The new computers were very successful, even exceeding the company's expectations. However, because of its success, IBM suddenly found itself needing more employees—especially engineers—to support the new product. And so a wave of new hiring began.

At the time, IBM Kingston was one of many plants and laboratories competing nationwide for top people. It wasn't long before our communications department was asked to help in the effort. The personnel department wanted us to write a brochure and produce a motion picture film that would highlight the Kingston site and the quality of life in the mid-Hudson Valley.

I was asked to write the film script and immediately began talking to people for input. One IBM employee (and a pilot on the weekends) suggested I check out the Old Rhinebeck Aerodrome in Rhinebeck, New York, across the river from Kingston. He said that the aerodrome was unique—a colorful throw-back to the barnstorming days of aviation. Moreover, the aerodrome was attracting lots of people.

Cole Palen, the founder of the aerodrome and a pilot himself, flew several of his vintage airplanes in weekend air shows during the summer. He and other pilots also took people up for rides. As the crowds increased, the aerodrome attracted a few other pilots who lived in the area and who were fascinated with the notion of flying and working on the historic airplanes.

We produced the film, and the old airplanes provided some of the best scenes. I couldn't help thinking about the coincidence of working on a film subject that so enthralled me as a kid. And the fact that the aerodrome was so close to our home was not lost on me either.

I was pretty sure that one day, Judy and I would fly in one of those planes. But there was no hurry. After all, we could do it almost any time in the summer months. The aerodrome would always be there.

However, years later, our world changed when we moved because I had a new job at IBM headquarters, in Armonk, NY. Any thoughts of flying in a biplane had to be put on hold.

Decades later, after taking early retirement from IBM, I added flying in a biplane to my list of things that I wanted to do while I was still able.

Eventually Judy and I returned to the Kingston area, where two of our three children were still living. During the summer of our first year back, we began to catch up on some of the promises we had made years earlier. Of course one of them was to fly in that biplane.

It was a beautiful, fall morning, and after a fifteen-year absence, Judy and I were finally going up in a 1929 New Standard DXXV biplane at the Old Rhinebeck Aerodrome.

Thirty or forty people were walking around the aerodrome that day, looking at the old planes. Vintage airplane buffs and pilots, dedicated to keeping such planes functioning, worked on two of the planes. Money from the admission fees and airplane rides helped pay for restoration and maintenance costs at the aerodrome.

Our pilot, Mike Lawrence, a veteran of over a thousand biplane flights, sauntered over to us. Tall and well-tanned, he had a ready smile and confident manner. We shook hands.

"This your first ride in a biplane?" he asked casually.

"Yes," we answered, almost in unison.

"Well, it's pretty straight-forward," Mike said. "We'll be running down this section of the airfield (pointing to a long, slanting hill) until we reach enough speed to become airborne. Being the nice day it is today, we'll cross the river (Hudson River), and you'll see some of Dutchess County (where the aerodrome was) and Ulster County (where we lived)."

There were two passenger seats behind Lawrence's cockpit. Judy sat directly behind him, and I sat behind her.

After we put on our seat belts, Lawrence started the motor. The noise from the 220-horsepower Continental radial engine was deafening. And it only got louder. Just when I thought something was going to blow, the plane began to move down the hill. We moved slowly at first, then faster and faster—as if Mike was trying to capture every bit of thrust possible. We rolled and rolled with great exuberance down the grassy hill.

When it looked as though we were going to roll into the river, the biplane left the ground gently like a feather in the wind. The upper and lower wings quickly stabilized at seventy miles an hour and an altitude of about one thousand feet, where we would stay for the ride. With takeoff safely behind us, we could relax and enjoy the sights below.

The initial view was out of a *National Geographic* magazine. We could see palettes of seasonal colors from the foliage on both sides of the majestic Hudson River. Equally striking was the graceful Rhinecliff Bridge that connected the Dutchess and Ulster counties.

Everything looked different from the air. Homes and landscapes took on qualities of neatness and purpose from above. They looked organized, logical, and beautiful.

That was particularly true when we saw the stately and historic homes that line the Hudson River in Dutchess County. I spotted the home where Gore Vidal, the writer, had lived for many years; the Vanderbilt Mansion; and, to the south, Franklin Delano Roosevelt's home and library.

I could see that Judy was busily looking out her windows, swiveling her head to the best views. We could see the New York State Thruway gracefully weaving its way through the state and Ashokan Reservoir—which supplies New York City with much of its drinking water. Behind the landmarks was a magnificent panorama of the Catskill Mountains.

Our eighteen-minute flight was over too quickly, of course, and on our way back to the airport, Judy turned around to look at me. She had a big grin on her face and her thumb was up. She obviously liked the ride.

We landed smoothly and thanked Lawrence for a great experience. And while I can't prove it, I think the smiles we wore after landing stayed with us for the rest of that day.

Up close

ANTARCTICA

When Judy and I first left the security of our Russian icebreaker to board a fourteen-foot Zodiac rubber raft in the Antarctic Ocean, we knew this trip would be different from any we had ever taken. We had to climb down a twenty-five-foot steel ladder outside the boat to a small metal platform that extended over the frigid water. From there we were to step—or jump, if necessary—into one of four bobbing Zodiacs. Three crewmen helped us. One was on the platform and one in the raft, while the pilot kept the bobbing raft as close to the platform as possible. Each of us had to step into the raft at the right moment—when it was closely aligned with the platform.

I was on deck waiting my turn to board, watching other passengers get into the raft. Most of them were doing OK, but some needed help. As ocean swells increased, a few people lost their balance and tumbled into the raft. But no harm done.

Then a heavy-set, middle-aged man stepped up. He seemed apprehensive. Just as he made his move, a large swell rolled in under the raft, elevating it above the platform. He suddenly lost his footing and fell, landing on the side of the Zodiac. To everyone's horror, he began to slide into the water between the raft and the ship. The alert boatman quickly grabbed the man's life jacket and held on to it until others in the raft came to his aid, pulling the now panicked man into the raft and safety. He was shaken up but uninjured.

Judy and I were on South Georgia, a small island in the Atlantic Ocean, on a voyage to Antarctica. Our expedition included thirty-eight people from around the world—most from the United States. The voyage would provide a special look into a world far beyond our daily experience.

Antarctica is an ice-buried continent that surrounds the South Pole. This nearly barren land covering 5.4 million square miles is the coldest and iciest region in the world. It's larger than either Europe or Australia and has ninety percent of the world's fresh water, in the form of ice. Stormy waters of the Atlantic, Indian, and Pacific oceans isolate Antarctica from other continents, and ships must carefully steer around towering icebergs to get there. On land, gigantic glaciers move imperceptibly downhill toward the sea. High mountain peaks and a few bare, rocky areas make up the only visible land. Temperatures rarely reach above thirty-two degrees Fahrenheit, and on July 21, 1983, scientists recorded the world's lowest temperature—minus 128.6 degrees Fahrenheit. Downright chilly.

Our nineteen-day odyssey began in January, summer in Antarctica, with an evening flight from Miami on Lan Chilé Airlines to

Santiago, Chilé. We arrived the following morning and transferred to the Hotel Carrera for an overnight stay.

A cocktail reception at the hotel that evening allowed us meet our traveling companions, an eclectic group of twenty women and eighteen men, ranging in age from mid-twenties to late sixties. Among them were a computer programmer from Colorado, a lighting wholesaler and his wife from California, a school teacher from Italy, an entrepreneur from Miami, and an attorney from Canada.

The next morning we flew over the snow-covered Andes to Ushuaia (oosh WHY ah), Argentina, the world's most southern city. From there, we would board our boat, the *MV Professor Multanovskiy*. The 236-foot ship was a steel, ice-strengthened vessel with a Russian crew. It was leased by Mountain Travel-Sobek, our tour company. Judy and I had a cabin with two berths, a writing desk, two small closets, a few built-in drawers, and, happily, a porthole through which we could view the world.

After leaving port, we were briefed in the ship's dining room by Jonathon Chester, our expedition leader. One of Australia's most experienced mountaineers and Antarctic explorers, Chester is also a renowned photographer and writer who has published several books on Antarctica. He described the daily routine we could expect on ship and on land and introduced his staff of seven, including naturalist-guides who would be lecturing and showing video tapes about the continent's geology, ecosystem, birds, animals, and history. We were also told that we could visit the bridge any time during the voyage, an offer that most of us would take up in the days ahead.

The Antarctic Ocean is sometimes called the Southern Ocean, and it is formed by the merging of the southern reaches of the Atlantic, Indian, and Pacific oceans. Our first port of call would be South Georgia, first accurately placed on the map by Captain James Cook in 1775. Our landing would be at Grytviken, which was the center of the southern hemisphere's whaling industry for over fifty years. The island of South Georgia is also where, in 1916, Sir Ernest Shackleton and a handful of men finished an epic eight hundred-mile journey from Elephant Island in a lifeboat. His ship, the *Endurance,* had been crushed by ice, forcing Shackleton and his crew to abandon ship. They would have perished on Elephant Island were it not for Shackleton using the lifeboat to get help before their provisions ran out. Many consider his heroic rescue of the crew to be the single greatest feat in the history of polar exploration.

Since Ushuaia was 1,100 miles from South Georgia, many of us decided to catch up on some sleep. Our first night went well. Judy and I dug out a few books to read, and lay down on our bunks. With smooth seas and the ship's slow rolling motion, sleep came quickly.

Our Russian crew served a buffet breakfast at eight o'clock. Judy and I had orange juice, scrambled eggs, sausage, toast, and coffee. The Russians were friendly, efficient, and good-humored. They spoke some English and seemed genuinely interested in trying to help us with such things as dietary needs, directions on board ship, and securing a cabinet door that swung back and forth in our cabin during rough weather.

After breakfast, many of us explored the ship, including the bridge. We watched sea birds and four dolphins that kept pace with the boat. It wasn't severely cold yet, but it was nippy. The wind was picking up on deck, but our bright red insulated jackets, supplied by Mountain Travel, kept us warm. Thankfully, we were going to Antarctica in the middle of its summer—December through February, a period that has sunlight twenty-four hours a day. Even so, we could feel it getting colder the farther south we went. We could only imagine what it would be like in winter—May through August—when temperatures range from minus ninety-four to minus forty degrees Fahrenheit.

We attended interesting lectures, usually including slides or videotapes, on the ship. The first day's included "Seabirds of the

Southern Ocean" and "Tips for Antarctic Photographers." Late in the afternoon, we had a surprise boat drill. Passengers and crew had to put on life jackets and head quickly to our assigned lifeboats. These boats were noticeably different than traditional lifeboats: They were totally enclosed and motorized—important considerations in sub-zero Antarctic waters.

The next morning, the wind picked up as we ran down the northern coast of South Georgia. It was cloudy, but we saw patches of blue above the snow-covered mountains that make up the backbone of the rugged island. We arrived at Grytviken (Grit-VI-ken) at noon and anchored at King Edward Point. There, a British garrison is quartered not far from the old whaling center. The weather was cold but not freezing when we embarked in our Zodiacs. We could see penguins on shore as we came in to dock.

Two British citizens—George Brown, who had wintered on the island as a radio operator from 1954 to 1957, and Pauline Carr, who ran the island's only museum and gift shop—met us. Some eighteen hundred tourists pass through Grytviken during the summer months to see the wildlife and the world's last whaling station.

We were fascinated by the museum's old photos of whaling operations and tools and artifacts used by whalers. Brown, who might have just stepped out of Hemingway's *The Old Man and the Sea*, gave us a tour of the rusting, abandoned factory where whales were stripped of their blubber—the fat from which oil is obtained—and anything else that could be sold. The late 1960s marked the end of the whaling industry simply because it became unprofitable due to new technologies. such as Power harpoon guns and factory ships that allowed the killing of more whales in less time than ever before all but decimated the world's whale population, killing an estimated 250,000 whales.

With three hours to explore South Georgia, we headed for the beach to check out the seals and penguins. We had seen pictures of elephant seals before but nothing could have prepared us for seeing them in the wild. A full-grown male can weigh over a ton and reach a length of twenty-one feet. They look like giant rock formations in the sand: unmovable, implacable. Elephant seals appear too sluggish to move quickly, but I discovered the hard way that appearances can be misleading. They can move, when threatened.

I wanted photos of a big bull sitting in the middle of his harem, so I had to get close. Approaching cautiously, I was about ten feet behind him, camera in hand, when he erupted with a bellow that could be heard back on the boat. His thick neck twisted angrily around to see what intruder was interrupting his afternoon of bliss. For a moment, I thought he was coming after me—despite his body being anchored in sand. I didn't think he could move quickly, but I wasn't sure. I decided to forego the shot and get out of there. Fast.

Penguin chick

We also saw our first type of penguin, King penguins. They were delightful. Four of them came to within six feet of Judy and me and just stood there staring at us. Healthy, adult penguins have no predators on land, so they have no fear of humans. Moreover, they're quite sociable. Other penguins began to join the group until we had ten or eleven penguins staring at us. Then I had an idea.

I slowly moved closer to them and lay down—resting on one arm on the ice, so I could see them—and waited. I didn't move. After a minute, one penguin walked over with a distinctive Charley Chaplin waddle and stood three feet away from me. I didn't move. I began talking to him quietly. Then the penguin—I called him Charley—moved closer and then, another penguin moved in.

And another.

By now, six curious penguins had waddled closer to watch the guy in the red coat. *Ah, the chorus has arrived,* I thought. Emboldened by his comrades, Charley now moved to within inches of my boot. To my surprise, he pecked it. I didn't move. He pecked it again. With each peck, the chorus moved closer as if to say, "Peck him again, Charley!"

In a gesture of friendship, I held out my hand as if to touch him, and that broke the spell. Charley turned around and imperiously waddled back to his original position, followed by the chorus. Then he paused and looked back at me. I spoke to him again, but he had had enough. Charley turned away again and waddled off.

Penguins are remarkable birds, often associated with Antarctica. They cannot fly but are skillful swimmers and can streak through the ocean diving for fish and other food. There are six kinds of penguins in Antarctica. Playful Adelie penguins are the most common. They build nests of pebbles on the shore. The taller, quieter Emperor penguin grows to about four feet. After the female emperor lays an egg on ice, the male rests the egg on his feet and warms it with the lower part of his belly. Chinstrap, Gentoo, King (like Charley), and Macaroni penguins nest on the peninsula and the islands. Some species spend as much as seventy-five percent of their lives in the ocean, yet they all breed on land or sea ice attached to land. All have similar streamlined bodies but vary in size. Their wings are highly modified, stiff, paddle-like flippers used for swimming. Their bones, solid and heavy, help them stay submerged, as needed for diving.

With a layer of blubber and a short, dense layer of feathers that form a waterproof coat, penguins are able to minimize heat loss in icy waters and withstand Antarctic blizzards.

Later that day, we saw Shackleton's burial site on a mountainside. It is marked by a simple stone cross, three feet high, which could be seen dramatically by ships coming to dock at South Georgia. We later read the original recruiting advertisement that Shackleton ran in London newspapers before his fateful voyage. Its message was prescient and blunt:

> Men wanted for hazardous duty, small wages, bitter cold, long months of complete darkness, constant danger, safe return doubtful. Honor and recognition in case of success.
> —Sir Ernest Shackleton

It was late when we boarded our Zodiaks and headed back to the ship, yet we were still excited from our day on South Georgia. After boarding, Judy and I headed for a shower and some rest before dinner. At 5:30 PM each day, coffee, tea, and snacks were available in one of the dining rooms. At 6:30 PM, happy hour began, continuing until 8:30 PM, when dinner was served. After dinner, people continued talking at their tables or attended movies in the lecture hall. Most of us, however, would call it a night and go to our cabins to recharge for the next day. Activities were well-planned so that everyone had a chance to meet other passengers.

We landed at various harbors and inlets on South Georgia over the next few days. Most of the landings were successful. Some were not.

The closer we got to Antarctica, the more unpredictable the weather became. Winds were getting stronger, as were the swells. One night we experienced forty-knot winds. The rocking of our ship loosened everything in our cabin. We slept very little that night.

Gold Harbour, on the southeast coast of South Georgia, was one of our most interesting landings. Even though we had size-able swells getting ashore, the variety of wildlife awaiting us was worth the effort. A guide estimated that we saw more than 100,000 King penguins. They were standing, staring, walking, and squawking, spread like a vast carpet of black and white from the shore to a magnificent glacier.

Chat time

"Incredible!" Judy said as she stared. It was like something from another world. We "red coats" began moving in among the penguins. They didn't seem to mind and moved out of our way only when they had to. They seemed as curious about us as we were about them.

Earlier in one of the lectures, we were advised to move slowly when observing the animals so as not to alarm them. It was good counsel and made our encounters more enjoyable.

We also saw fur seals. They are quite territorial and can be aggressive. Judy found that out when she inadvertently walked between a fur seal's nest on land and the ocean, thus cutting off its access to the water. I looked up to see my wife was running faster than I ever thought possible in all that gear. Right behind her was a young, barking fur seal in full pursuit.

"He's gaining on you Jude," I yelled, the ever helpful spouse. "Run faster!"

Once the fur seal chased her away from his path to the sea, he must have considered the threat neutralized and quit the chase. Judy would read later what she had already learned the hard way—that adult fur seals can out-run humans on a flat surface.

Adding more excitement to our day was a dramatic rendezvous with three young adventurers who, for the last two months, had been circumnavigating South Georgia in kayaks. It was a daunting task for anyone, given the uncertainties of South Georgia weather. They were lucky we were able to find them. They had encountered bad weather and had to camp on shore. One kayak was damaged, and they were low on food since the weather problem added extra days to their schedule.

The kayakers—Angus Finney and Wade Fairley from Australia and Bob Powell from North Carolina—had reservations for the trip back to Ushuaia. However, while we all got on at Ushuaia they—and their kayaks—boarded ship in South Georgia, in the middle of the Antarctic Ocean. They were bright, engaging young men looking for adventure around the world before settling down. I wondered later what would have happened to them if we had been unable to launch the Zodiacs for their rendezvous.

We were now getting closer to Antarctica. The smaller icebergs we had been seeing (berg-y bits) were now giving way to larger icebergs—some as much as fifteen thousand feet deep. It was also getting colder. Rounding the eastern tip of the South Orkney Islands, we saw Minke and Fin whales, seals, and thousands of penguins, many of them on icebergs. The scene reminded me of Roald Amundsen's initial impressions of Antarctica on his way to the South Pole. He wrote:

> Glittering white, shining blue, raven black, in the light of the sun, the land looks like a fairy tale, pinnacle after pinnacle, peak after peak crevassed, wild as any land on our globe, it lies unseen and untrodden.

As the sun glistened on icebergs, we finally landed on Antarctica at Brown Bluff. Penguins porpoised as if they were an official welcoming committee. Towering cliffs and boulder-strewn slopes provided a dramatic backdrop for the thousands of Adelie and Gentoo penguins nesting on shore. We spent hours studying their behavior and soaking up the vastness of Antarctic Sound, strewn with grounded icebergs as far as the eye could see. We marked the occasion with a champagne toast and a group photo. Then we got back in the Zodiacs and cruised among the icebergs and gazed at the ice-covered cliffs.

That afternoon, our ship continued south to Paulet Island where we saw the remains of the stone hut that housed Captain Carl Larsen and twenty-one sailors after they were marooned. Their ship, the *Antarctic,* had been crushed by ice twenty-three miles east of the island in 1903. Looking at their small, roofless hut, it was hard to image that many people living there under such difficult conditions for over a year before they were rescued.

The Penguin Bowl

Cruising among the icebergs, we came upon what looked like a frozen amphitheater, populated from top to bottom with hundreds of penguins. It was as beautiful as it was bizarre. All I could think of was the Hollywood Bowl. The penguins were standing around, as they do—in formal attire of course, and it wasn't hard to imagine that they were just waiting for their conductor.

The bowl-like iceberg on which they stood was slippery, and thirty or forty penguins were sliding into the water at any given time. Other penguins were trying to get up on the iceberg. It was tricky because a penguin has to build up enough momentum under water to thrust—or porpoise—its body out of the water and onto an iceberg landing spot. Adult penguins had it down pretty well, but the younger ones didn't. They would shoot out of the water, nowhere close to their target, defy gravity for a few seconds, then fall back into the ocean.

Sometimes penguins landed on the slick ice but slid back into the water because they were off balance. What made it so humorous was that there was so much of it going on at the same time. It was like a Keystone Comedy. We could have watched for hours.

At Hanna's Point, our last landing in the South Shetland Islands, we went to see the elusive Macaroni penguins. We had missed them earlier because of aborted landings due to weather. The name "macaroni" is derived from the eighteenth-century dandies who made the grand tour to Italy and affected continental tastes and fashions, dying their hair in yellow streaks.

Arriving back in England they were promptly called macaronis, like the Italian pasta. The Macaroni penguin has similar yellow streaks on their heads and are easily spotted.

It was raining and muddy when we got to the point, and conditions only got worse. When the rain turned to snow (in the middle of summer, yet), things really got messy. Finally, we found some Macaronis who looked as wet and bedraggled as we did. By then, the consensus of the group was to return to the ship.

The snow storm was a fitting reminder that nature was still in charge. Any visit to Antarctica is on nature's terms. And that's fair because we were privileged to visit a magical place. We shared the landscape with dozens of unique animal species, unafraid and unperturbed by our presence. We saw castles of ice and seas of glass—spectacular beauty that none of us will forget. Soon we'd be heading home, via the Drake Passage to Ushuaia, where our journey began—a journey to nature's last continent and most remote stronghold on the planet.

EPILOGUE

At this writing, it's clear that my original thirty-one goals will not all be reached.

That's OK. We'll remember the twenty-two that were. Judy and I may still make it to Australia, and, hopefully, I'll learn to play the piano better than I do now. We'll continue doing the best we can with the time we have, and if we reach a few more goals, that's fine. If we don't, that's OK too because we've already been rewarded far beyond anything we could have imagined two decades ago when this quest began.

During the early years of writing the book, I sent out a few chapters to some newspapers, just to see if the stories were publishable. I didn't have to wait long.

An editor from *The New Jersey Bergen Record*, a large daily newspaper, called asking if the paper could run the Kilimanjaro story in its Sunday edition. As a result of that story came another request, almost unbelievably, from *The New York Times* to run the story of the Kili climb written by their writer.

After the stories were published, our phone began to ring. We got calls from people who had read the stories and wanted us to speak before groups such as Rotary, Kiwanis, Lions, AARP, State University of New York, Elderhostel, and the like.

We were able to cobble together enough color slides from our trips to put together a thirty-minute talk. The talks were well-received and, more importantly, fun to do. We soon learned that there was a big audience out there of people fifty years and over who are living longer and looking for more stimulating outlets for themselves with the time they have left.

However, for us, there was a price to pay. The time and preparation required for the talks ground progress on the book virtually to a halt. We had to decide where our priorities were and get back to writing and finishing the book.

Now that the book is published, Judy and I can see ourselves continuing with the slide shows and talks wherever there's an interested audience. As I mentioned before, a good part of our payback would be the stimulation that we would get from an inter-active audience who might be looking for a little more adventure in their own lives.

We'll soon find out.

—DM

HOW to START

All too often, we muddle through life reacting to what we think we should do but not always doing what we want. Busy lifestyles often have a way of crowding out personal goals. One day we discover we're getting older and begin to wonder if it's too late to climb that tall mountain or run white-water rapids, as we once dreamed of doing.

The purpose of this chapter—as well as the book, for that matter—is to help make you aware of your own potential to extract more from life than the predictable, and to encourage you to do it while you still can. Your quest can involve reaching any number of your personal goals. Through planning and determination, you just might reach more of them than you ever thought possible.

Before giving up on any of your dreams, take a look at a simple four-step approach to answer your questions and, in the process, make your life more interesting.

FOUR-STEP APPROACH

1. WRITE DOWN YOUR GOALS.

2. GATHER INFORMATION ON EACH GOAL.

3. DEVELOP A PLAN.

4. START AN EXERCISE PROGRAM.

1. Write Down Your Goals

This is the easy part. Making a list formalizes your commitment, or at least your interest, to the goals that lie ahead. Your list should simply include some of the things you have long wanted to try but, for one reason or another, haven't done. You may not reach all of your goals, but that's OK, because there's a good chance you'll reach some of them.

In writing out your list, try to resist the urge to pre-edit or omit certain goals because you think they're too expensive, too dangerous, or would simply too time-consuming. This is a normal reaction, but at this stage, your intent should be just to get your ideas on paper. Later you can drop the truly unrealistic goals from the list.

Some years back, I thought that there was no way Judy and I could go to places like Africa, Antarctica, and Nepal. Such trips were beyond our means in both time and expense. But had we eliminated those goals early on, we would have trashed half our list and might never have made some amazing trips. And, just because Judy and I couldn't reach a particular goal anytime soon, that didn't mean we could *never* reach that goal. Who knows? Maybe in five or ten years your finances will improve. And who's to say that you won't have more available time at another stage of your life. Another reason to put your goals on paper.

In writing out your goals, find a quiet place where you're not likely to be disturbed. Also, realize that your list probably won't be finished in one or two sittings. More likely it will be on-going, so prepare to add or eliminate goals as you see fit.

As for the number of goals, that's up to you. There can be ten or 110—whatever you decide. For example, Lou Holtz, the former head football coach at the University of South Carolina and Notre Dame once told me that he had 107 goals on his list. They included such things as: Go on an African safari, hit a golf ball for a hole-in-one, and run with the bulls in Pamplona. Thanks but I'll skip the bulls in Pampalona, Lou.

2. Gather Information on Each Goal

After you've written your list, you need information about your goals. One way to begin is to contact some of the more than two hundred outfitters in the United States who organize trips to virtually every corner of the planet. A growing number of companies specialize in adventure travel, which has been booming over the last several decades. Most of these companies have toll-free numbers, which you can call to request catalogues with up-to-date information about such trips as white-water rafting, trekking, climbing, ballooning, canoeing, kayaking, cycling, etc. The catalogues also provide trip costs, dates of departure and return, the best times to go, etc.

After reading the catalogues, do some comparison shopping and write down the questions that you'd like answered. Then start calling the toll-free numbers to get more specific information. The telephone representatives are quite knowledgeable and will be able to answer most of your questions. If they can't, they'll find someone who can.

For example, I had a number of questions I wanted to ask about climbing Mount Kilimanjaro, such as the best time to go, the degree of difficulty, and how best to train. I also asked my rep at Abercrombie & Kent (A&K), "Could you get me the phone number of someone in my age bracket (I was fifty-nine at the time) who has climbed Kilimanjaro and who could tell me personally about the problems he or she encountered?"

The rep called back the following day with the name and phone number of a fifty-seven year-old-attorney in Chicago who had been on Kili several months earlier. She called him, told him about my request, and got his permission to give me his phone number. I called the next day, and he was very helpful as to what

I could expect on the climb. I asked him a number of questions about the difficulties he encountered, asking what he would do differently if he did it again. He gave me very good information, and based on his comments, I decided to make the climb.

3. Develop a Plan

Once you have your list, start thinking about priorities. What should I do first? Can I afford it? How much time will it take? How should I prepare?

When one reflects upon his or her lifespan, patterns emerge, major events that reinforce the adage: There's a time and place for everything.

There is a time to be born, go to school, get a job, marry, raise a family, and retire. These are time windows, as it were.

When you think about it, a trip to another continent to climb a tall mountain or run some serious white-water rapids is not exactly a routine event. As with any other major life event, such trips also are important and require planning and preparation.

Perhaps the most important consideration of all—especially with adventure travel—is your health and physical condition. If your list includes a goal with a high degree of difficulty, you should find out—well in advance of the trip.

Adventure travel trips can be expensive. In our case, Judy and I could not afford expensive trips while our three kids were still in college. Some of the trips had to wait until the kids were out of school or I had retired.

But having a plan was helpful. After making and researching our list, we had a good idea about the best times to take our trips and how much money we would have to save for them.

In planning major trips, don't overlook goals that can be reached closer to your home or that can be done on weekends or vacations from work. A number of my goals, such as parachuting, flying a glider, scuba diving, and parasailing were reached in this manner.

4. Start an Exercise Program

If any of your goals are strenuous, know that you will have to get into good physical condition. That should be your number one goal. Don't wait. Also, realize that the younger you are, the more likely you are to reach the more difficult goals. Whenever possible, go for the tougher goals, such as climbing and white-water rafting, first. The more fit you are, of course, the better your chance of reaching your goals.

Before starting any vigorous exercise program, it's a good idea to check with your doctor. If he agrees with your plan, consider joining a health club or a YMCA and working with a trainer to develop a plan, set targets for you and monitor your workouts.

Eating the right food and liquids is also important to getting into condition. When we decided to get in shape we cut out most of the fat in our diet and replace it with protein, veggies, and fruit. Before a workout, a slice of natural turkey tastes good and is high in protein. When hiking, we always take snacks of fruit, baggies of "gorp" (or trail mix), nuts, and dried fruit like raisins. We prefer all-natural products that are readily available in health food stores and many markets. Be careful of added sugar and salt. We also like small carrots that are sweet, crisp, and sturdy for traveling. To drink, there's nothing better than water, perhaps with some added lemon juice. Try to avoid cola drinks.

Health clubs are great, but if you enjoy swimming, biking, jogging, hiking, or walking and are self-disciplined to exercise on your own, by all means develop a routine that you like. The most effective exercise plan is one you will do regularly, at least two or three days a week.

IF YOU GO

Adventure travel has virtually exploded over the last several decades, and that means competition, which gives us all more choices. In this chapter, we'll give you a list of some of the outfitters who are in this business—including a few that Judy and I have worked with over the years.

Their trip specialists are well informed and will send you itemized check lists for the trip you are interested in, including types of clothing suggested for that climate and miscellaneous items that you might need.

For some trips, keep in mind that there are places where you can *rent* items you may not want to purchase, such as things you feel you'd never use again. We rented special boots for Antarctica and the super heavy clothing needed for dog sledding.

If the trip requires leaving the country, the travel companies can send you material on medical information required for that destination, such as vaccinations, malaria pills, etc. Travel groups also know what visas are needed and the best way to obtain them.

Perhaps you're concerned about signing up for a trip that might be too physically demanding or, on the other hand, not challenging enough. Each trip is usually rated on a scale from one to five, one being the easiest and five the most difficult. Your travel representative can be helpful in interpreting the rankings and leading you to the appropriate trip.

Adventure Travel Groups We've Used

Abercrombie & Kent (Africa)
    A&K
    1-800-323-7308
    1520 Kensington Road
    Oak Brook, IL 60523
    www.abercrombiekent.com

Mountain Travel-Sobek
    1-888-687-6235
    1266 66th Street, Suite 4
    Emeryville, CA 94608
    www.mtsobek.com

Outdoor Adventure River Specialists
    OARS
    1-800-346-6277
    PO Box 67
    Angels Camp, CA 95222
    www.oars.com

Wintergreen—Dog Sledding
    1-800-584-9425
    1101 Ring Rock Road
    Ely, MN 55731
    www.wintergreen.com

Parachuting

There are a number of parachute centers in the United States and abroad. We've listed a central Web site for the United States and a few companies on different coasts to get you started. Be sure to check that the center you're dealing with has an annual license from the commissioner of transportation.

General web site: www.parachutecenter.com

Skydive Newport
    Newport State Airport
    Middletown, RI 02842
    1-877-723-6423
    www.skydivenewport.com

Parachute Center
    P.O. Box 423
    23579 N. Hwy 99
    Acampo, CA 95220
    1-209-369-1182
    www.parachutecenter.com

Cleveland Parachute Center, Inc.
    15199 Grove Road
    Garrettsville, OH 44231
    1-800-522-5867

Directory of Travel Groups

The following list includes travel groups for trekking, bicycling, dog sledding, etc. You should be able to plan any trip with the list on this page.

Above the Clouds Trekking 1-800-233-4499
Adventure Canada 1-800-363-7566
Alaska Discovery 1-800-586-1911
AARP 1-888-687-2277
Backcountry 1-800-575-1540
Backroads (bicycling) 1-800-584-9425
Baja Expeditions 1-800-843-6967
Bike Treks International 1-800-300-1565
Bolder Adventures 1-800-642-2742
Earth Watch 1-800-776-0188
Elderhostel 1-877-426-8056
Esplanade Tours 1-800-628-4893
Guides for all Seasons 1-800-457-4574
International Expeditions 1-800-633-4734
Marine Expeditions 1-800-263-9147
Mountain Madness 1-800-328-5925
Nature Expeditions International 1-800-869-0639
Nature Quest 1-800-369-3033
The Northwest Passage 1-800-732-7328
Pacific Coast Adventures 1-800-491-3483
Quark Expeditions 1-800-356-5699
See & Sea Travel 1-800-348-9778
Society Expeditions 1-800-548-8669
Southwind Adventures 1-800-377-9463
Voyagers International 1-800-633-0299
Wilderness River Outfitters 1-800-252-6581

978-0-595-41015-6
0-595-41015-4

Printed in the United States
72034LV00002B/505-522